Writing Kidlit 102:
Your First Draft

Writing Kidlit 102:
Your First Draft

Victoria J. Coe

Cheryl Lawton Malone

Write On Productions

Boston

Write On Productions, LLC, Boston, MA

First published in the United States by Write On Productions, 2024

Text copyright © 2024 by Victoria J Coe and Cheryl Lawton Malone

Cover design copyright © 2024 by Wallace West

All Rights Reserved.

Write On Productions supports copyright. Copyright fuels creativity, encourages diverse voices, promotes free speech, and creates a vibrant culture. Thank you for buying and authorized edition of this book and for complying with copyright laws by not reproducing, scanning, or distributing any part of it in any form without written permission.

THE LIBRARY OF CONGRESS HAS CATALOGUED THIS EDITION AS FOLLOWS:
Coe, Victoria J. and Malone, Cheryl Lawton
p. cm.
Summary: "A self-guided, workbook-style course designed to facilitate writing a first draft of children's and young adult fiction." – Provided by the publisher.
ISBN 979-8-9876665-2-4
[Creative writing – Juvenile fiction.]
I. Title
LCCN 2023933788
[Non Fic] – 808.068

The content of this book is the original work of the authors. Similarities to other published material is entirely coincidental, unless otherwise noted within the text.

Dedication

To everyone who's ever had

a love/hate relationship

with a first draft.

—VJC & CLM

Contents

Hello 1
   Here's the Skinny
   Take a Breath – Just Write!

Session 1 — Set Yourself Up for Success 5
   Mommy, Where Do Ideas Come From?
   R&D
   Mentor Texts
   Your Tool Box
   Take a Breath – Mindset, Goals, & Accountability

Session 2 — Find Your "Just Right" Approach 21
   There's No Right Way to Write
   Smorgasbord, Anyone?
   Take a Breath – Yikes! Fear and How to Overcome It

Session 3 — This Is How WE Do it! 31
   Prewriting
   The Big 3
   The Unspoken Story Question & Emotional Arc
   The 5 Turns
   Take a Breath – Oh No! Writer's Block

Session 4 — Get Started 51
   A Scene by Any Other Name...
   Curtain Up – Opening Scenes
   Planning Ahead
   Take a Breath – Later, Gator... Procrastination

Session 5 — Keep Going 71
   Curtain Down – Closing Scenes
   Digging Deeper – Subplots
   The Messy Middle
   Take a Breath – Holy Moley, Now What?

And... That's a Wrap 91

Appendix – Outline: *Agnes and Tofu and the Best Paws Detective Agency*

Hello!

Whether you've worked your way through *Writing Kidlit 101* or this is your first time with us, welcome to *Writing Kidlit 102: Your First Draft*.

Writing a book – no matter how long or short – is a challenge. Sure, you could just sit down and let the words flow out of you. But the reality is – except for a lucky few – 1st drafts rarely come about that way.

That's where we come in.

Between us, we've written loads of stories for kids and young adults. More than a dozen made it to publication. Over 350,000 copies of our books are currently on bookshelves and in libraries around the world.

We each started with a simple dream – to write books for kids. While juggling careers and raising kids, we spent a ton of time educating ourselves, reading, getting advice, and of course, writing.

You probably won't be surprised that each of our published books took many, many drafts and in some cases YEARS of revision to get them into shape. But here's something that might surprise you – all that revising wasn't the hardest part. Not even close. Wanna guess what was?

The 1st draft. 100%.

Because in your 1st draft, you have to decide: Where to start? What to say? How to say it? How to find momentum? How to keep it? How to stop sabotaging yourself? Those frustrated feelings have been hard to forget. (Can you tell?)

Skip forward to today.

Although at heart we're writers, we're also teachers. We've taught hundreds of people like you how to navigate the writing process. And we've learned a TON along the way. We're talking a literal TON. And what we want you to know is there's no "one way" to write a picture book or novel. Even from author to author, the process can change. It usually does!

What we love to help with – and honestly, what matters – is finding the process that works for you, and then keeping you motivated. That's why we created this course – to help you nail down your story idea, your characters, and your plot, then start writing a workable – notice we didn't say PERFECT – 1st draft, and lastly but most importantly, FINISH!

In other words, we want to help you write the draft that will launch your story.

While our earlier book *Writing Kidlit 101* isn't a 100% prerequisite for this one, please note that we assume you're acquainted with the essentials we covered in that book. So, if you need a boost when we talk about today's kidlit marketplace, creating characters, building a world, finding your voice, writing dialogue, raising stakes, creating antagonists, telling a story (vs building a plot), understanding scenes, pacing, and structure, feel free to refer to *Writing Kidlit 101* for explanations, nuance, context, and refreshers.

Of course, we're sticking with our brand. We want you to wrangle that story out of your heart. On your terms. In your time. And in your way.

So please, think of this course as a how-to on starting your 1st draft and writing straight through to THE END, including some necessary breathing room to keep you on track. Because the most elusive prize of all – your forever-heart story – is calling to be fleshed out and put on paper. Like, now.

Here's the Skinny

This self-paced course is divided into 5 sessions – Set Yourself Up for Success, Find Your "Just Right" Approach, This Is How WE Do It, Get Started, and Keep Going.

Session 1, Set Yourself Up for Success, is a deep dive into honing your idea, doing research, checking out mentor texts, and navigating the world of writing tools.

A word of warning – in case you want to jump straight to Session 4, Get Started, hold back!

> We usually say the opposite, right? Typically, we're all about going at your own pace. Writing the way that works for you. This is our ONLY exception! Spending time on Sessions 1 – 3 now, WILL pay off later. We promise!

In Session 2, Find Your "Just Right" Approach, we share a bunch of drafting methods that many writers use. As we said above, you could try sitting down and letting the words flow (and keep flowing until you get to the end). That's one method for sure, and it does work for some. But if that's not you – psst, it's not us either – there's no need to reinvent the wheel. We show you how other writers have successfully written their books in all different ways.

Of course, in Session 3, This is How WE Do It, we devote a ton of real estate to OUR WAY, which includes Prewriting, the Big 3, the Big 3 Plus One (the unspoken story question) and the 5 Turns – the approach we humbly think is the easiest and most practical.

Are you surprised? Hey, this is OUR BOOK!

Then, in Session 4, Get Started, we'll teach you how to write your 1st draft, starting with breaking down your story into scenes (hint: your story, no matter how short, is a series of scenes). Don't know what a scene is? No worries. Not only do we explain the idea, but we also give examples! Then we'll guide you through your story's opening scene without rewriting it 10,000 times. Trust us, starting with a workable opening (think: not perfect – remember, this is a 1st DRAFT) is all that you need. And lastly, we'll help you see your story as a whole so you can plan and write the rest.

Finally, in Session 5, Keep Going, we point out that 1st drafts don't always follow the plan. When technical issues arise – and they will – we offer advice and techniques on how to fix the problem(s). For added value, we also note how the fixes can ease you back into your story if you find yourself at a stop. Session 5 starts with the crazy idea of writing your ending immediately after your beginning (read on!), and includes clever ways to weave in subplots, push your way through the messy middle, and do all the things that will get you through to the end.

In other words, we've got you all the way! AND... (Yes, there's more!)

Remember the breathing room we mentioned above? At the end of each of the five sessions, we build in the opportunity for self-reflection. We call these sections Take a Breath, and they offer exactly that: a breather from the hard task of preparing to write and then writing.

The Take a Breath sections are designed to help you face the well-known mental challenges that stalk the writing process. Some serve up motivational activities to overcome your fears and re-engage if you're disengaged. Others include tips and exercises to catch you up if you're behind and/or push you forward if you're blocked.

If we say so ourselves, we LOVE our Take A Breaths! Because who doesn't need help holding yourself accountable? Or kicking fear and writer's block to the curb? Or calling out your procrastinating self? We know our breathing sections work because we've been there! Many times!

So, find the sections that speak to you. Spend as much time as you need . . . uh oh. . . that was a test. Because spending *too* much time on any one aspect of writing – even something as beneficial as getting your head on straight – can turn into . . . PROCRASTINATION! LOL. Get it?

Okay, enough introduction. (Drum roll, please) We're thrilled to offer our very first Take a Breath section: Just Write.

Because that's what you're here to do. And you're itching to get started. We can feel it.

Take a Breath
Just Write!

Write 10 opening lines.
Opening lines to what?
It doesn't matter. The goal of this exercise is to get you started.

> Once upon a time, there lived a turtle who was pink.
> The Hairy Fairy had 3 favorite foods – dandelion salad, sugar soup, and green beetle stew.
> Everything about that day was a disaster until we found the charm.

Get it? Anything goes. Just write. Now. 10 lines. Go!

– Session 1 –
Set Yourself Up for Success

Mommy, Where Do Stories Come From?

Everybody knows that stories come from the stork! And by STORK, we mean YOUR IMAGINATION. If you're 100% dialed in with your story idea – we're talking the one that gives you – you pick: shivers, goosebumps, that "it" feeling – by all means, skip ahead to the section on R&D. If not, or if you're not sure, read on.

Maybe you have so many ideas, you don't know which one to write first. Or when it comes to ideas, you've got a whole lotta nothin'. Or maybe you're somewhere in the middle (see us raising our hands?).

No matter how easy – or hard – it is for you to grab an idea, we've got you. Here are some tried-and-true ways to think up story ideas. Give them a shot and see what works for you! Because it's better to start with one idea and change your mind than to never start at all.

Get Inspired by the Marketplace

Do some recon at your local library. Talk to children's librarians. Ask for NEW BOOKS in your category and genre (Category, think: picture book, middle grade, or YA.

Genre, think: realism, fantasy, adventure, humor – you get the idea.) Go through the recs. What intrigues you? (Just so you know, it's totally okay to borrow books from the kids' section. We do it all the time.)

Do the same at the bookstore, preferably an indie bookstore that supports authors like Future You. Ask what books they just sold in your category and genre. Old or new. Buy them if you can, but definitely jot down the title and research the book when you get home. What do you notice about the books that are selling today? Do any of your observations speak to you?

What If...?

Mash up ideas. What if *Star Wars* mashed up with *The Little Engine That Could*? What if *Little Red Riding Hood* and *The Shirley Chisholm Story* had a "baby?" What if you mixed up *Goodnight Moon* and *The Giver*? (Just to be clear – we're not recommending any of these!) We *are* encouraging you to think in new and interesting ways.

Get outside and move your body! There's no better way to open your brain to new "what ifs" than taking a bike ride or a walk. The point is that ideas can come from anywhere. The woods. Clouds. The sign in a store window. Pop culture, social media, and news stories, too. Look at anything and everything around you and ask, "What if...?"

Give a familiar story a "what if" twist. What if Romeo met a boy named Contro before he met Juliet? What if Cinderella were a dog? What if Humpty Dumpty fell but didn't crack his shell?

Get good at playing the "what if" game. The possibilities are endless. Let your mind wander. No matter how many ideas you have, pick one to work on first. If you can't choose your fave, phone a friend and ask them. Preferably a friend who reads in your category, or even a kid.

Sir Mix-a-Lot

Or try the "mix and match" game. (Can you tell we love games – or at least one of us does?)

Step 1. Make a list of characters. Let your mind go wild. Human, animal, object. Different ages, genders, backgrounds. Realistic or fantastical worlds.

Step 2. Make a list of wants. Fears. Threats. Goals your characters want but can't achieve. In *Writing Kidlit 101*, we refer to this WANT as the story problem, what your character wants – badly. The story problem is the foundation for your action plot.

Step 3. Connect each character to a problem.

Character	Story Problem
Toba, the anteater	Gets lost at sea
Ficus, an orphan	Loses a magic watch
Clemmy, a drug addict	Is accused of murder

Cross lines. Double back. Connect dots. There are at least 64 different story ideas here (Nerd alert – think Pascal's Triangle). Which one intrigues you?

Your Character/Story Problem table is a living, breathing document. Keep it handy. Look at it often. Especially if your last idea was meh (we promise we're not judging).

When a story idea does speak to you, ask yourself, "Why?" Why is that character afraid of that thing? Why is that threat a problem for the character? Why does the character desire that goal, and more importantly, who or what is getting in their way? The story of your heart is in there somewhere. We know it. And you know it.

Stranger Than Fiction

Let ideas find you. Think of your own childhood or high school years. Read blogs and listen to podcasts that kids in your category are into. Notice the issues that kids or teens in your life are grappling with. Open yourself up to real situations. Look. Listen. Imagine. One of us regularly hunts through *National Geographic* for story ideas from nature.

Now go back to that list. Character/Story Problem. If making this list becomes a habit, kudos. You'll be shocked at how many go-to story ideas you'll have.

> Pro tip: Don't be too literal about turning a true story into fiction. Use it as inspiration. As a jumping off point. But don't try to tell it exactly as it happened. It hardly ever works – unless you want to write nonfiction. (And if you do, GO FOR IT.)

Understand that some ideas work. Others don't. Don't be discouraged when something you thought was amazing turns out to be ugh.

Could This Idea Be THE ONE?

When you get an idea that you like, give it time to sink in. Let it take over your imagination. Scribble thoughts as they come to you. Wrap your head around it. Do you really love it? Are you willing to spend the next 6 months – or 6 years – writing about it?

Does your idea lead you to another more interesting idea? Do your thoughts start to build on each other?

When you literally can't stop thinking about it, you've found THE ONE.

But wait, seriously? Is there really a single story that will become your soulmate? Maybe, yes. Maybe, no. The point is – you won't know until you write it.

R&D

Research and Development? Yup. Even for realistic fiction? YES.

Is your character a budding gymnast? A hockey player? A chess champ? The youngest in a large family? A kid dealing with alopecia? No matter who your character is, your reader expects them to feel REAL. Even if they are a literal unicorn or a fairy or a unicorn fairy. So DO find your characters' counterparts in real life – or as close as you can get – and research them until you know everything about them.

Does your story take place in a real location, like the elementary school in your neighborhood, a small town in rural Oklahoma, or a city like Cleveland or San Diego? What about the Gelato Galaxy? If so, comb through the real location or its closest equivalent until you can lead a tour. DYK (Did you know): Fantasy worlds are often based on real places – be they land, ocean, or space?

Maybe your story takes place during a real historic event, like the famous earthquake that rocked the 1989 World Series in San Francisco. But in your story, the earthquake is caused by an invasion force from Pluton 9, a science experiment gone wrong, or a game of stick ball played by monsters.

Whatever! You can add authenticity by reading accounts of the 1989 quake, making a Pinterest photo board of the old Candlestick Park, visiting the site if you can, and related museums (IRL or virtually). Read whatever archives and interviews are available. Take notes on the tangible details – the smells, the tastes, the sounds of that extraordinary time, politics, pop culture – you get the idea.

It's so easy to do research these days – besides Google, Pinterest, and YouTube, don't overlook OG research at the library or interviewing experts. Arm yourself with enough info (think: not an encyclopedia's worth) so your characters, your plot, and your setting feel authentic.

Mentor Texts

Mentor texts are books you love and maybe wish you'd written yourself. A great mentor text has a theme, character, structure, OR a story problem LIKE yours. Notice we didn't say AND.

We use mentor texts for research, for inspo, and for the sheer love of reading. We can't think of a single story we've written that hasn't first started with a search for mentor texts – even if they're old classics.

Wait. Wait. Wait. Didn't we hammer home how different books are today in our first book, *Writing Kidlit 101*? How irrelevant older stories are for today's readers? You bet we did.

And we hope this isn't confusing. Because before you start writing your totally relevant, super cool story that today's kids want to read – it can help to peek back at old faves in your category as learning tools. Mentor texts can come from anywhere, as long as you use them in the right way.

The point of using mentor texts is to learn. To be inspired. How did that other writer present their story? Forgetting whether that book would or wouldn't make it today, how did that writer hit their theme – mental health, coming of age, loneliness, finding friends, sibling rivalry? Obviously? Subtly? Does the theme show up on page 1?

How did they deal with technical details – dialogue on page 1? Tons of interior thought? Hardly any? What about stakes? And heart?

And BTW, mentor texts can absolutely overlap with comps – think: comparable titles, ie recently published books (within 1 to 3 years) that are similar to yours, and yet different enough so that your story stands out in the marketplace.

But they don't HAVE TO overlap. For example, a book published in 2010 might not (would not!) be a great comp but might be a fantastic mentor text for a certain aspect of your story.

Here's an easy roadmap to finding your mentor texts.
- Identify your category: Picture book, Middle Grade, YA.
- Narrow down your genre; adventure, humor, contemporary, fantasy…
- Identify up to 3 themes in YOUR story: friendship, fitting in, coming of age…
- Take your category, genre, and main theme from above, say YA, contemporary, fitting in, and run them through your favorite book sites like Goodreads and Amazon as if they were SEO words. See what pops up.
- Order those results from your library or bookstore.
- Read! Observe! Make notes. Enjoy!

One final thought – ANY book can be a mentor text if there's something there that inspires you. It doesn't have to be from your category or genre at all.

Say you want to write about a 10-year-old girl who's obsessed with competitive gymnastics. And you're reading an adult romance where you're truly amazed at how well the author conveys the main character's obsession with competitive fishing. Take note of how the author does that.

See what you can learn and how that might apply to your story. Get it?

Your Toolbox

The only tools you NEED to write a book are a laptop, tablet, or a phone. Or if you're old school: pen and paper.

But we'd like to introduce you to some extra tools – at all price points – that just might become your new bffs. (Some of them are definitely ours!)

We promise we're not trying to complicate the writing process – au contraire! Tools can help you see your story at a glance, which literally makes writing simpler. Really.

Here are some of our fave tools. Try the ones that appeal to you.

PB Dummies

For picture books, our favorite tool is called a dummy, which is a thumbnail sketch of each page in your story. But whoa, SKETCH? What if you can't draw?

You don't need to! The dummy is not about art. It's about mapping out the story and being able to see how it unfolds at a glance. (Of course, if you ARE an author-illustrator, feel free to load your dummy up with art, doodles, sketches, and whatever else you want!)

> Pro tip: Many writers hold off on creating their PB dummies until after they've written a worthy (insert air quotes) draft to confirm layout, page breaks, and to plug in the text on the appropriate page – or if you're an author-illustrator – text and illustrations. Which is awesome! There's nothing like a PB dummy to point out those cringe-worthy bare spots, horrible-snoozy sections, and spreads with are-you-kidding-me? Way-too-much-text! The beauty is, you can find those flaws in the privacy of your own space BEFORE you show your manuscript to others.
>
> But that's the point, isn't it? Dummies are SO great at pointing out weaknesses, we think you should use them to write your 1st draft! In other words, dummies are not just for page turns! Seriously. There is no better tool to tease out character, plot, arcs, and pacing. Why wait until you're finished?

Great, you say. I'm in. How do I start?

The old school way to create a dummy is to stack 8 ½ x 11-inch paper pages and staple them together like an actual book. Or using note cards or post-its, arrange them on the wall or table (or hey, the floor). Or draw squares on a white board or a big sheet of paper.

Techies can simulate a picture book by using a software program or creating cells in a spreadsheet like Google sheets or Excel that visually resemble the open pages of a picture book. Or download a picture book dummy template online. Or paste a series of boxes into your word processing program. Whatever works, works.

Following the handy guide below, make sure your software template (or cards or squares or boxes) totals 32 pages – the length of a traditional picture book.

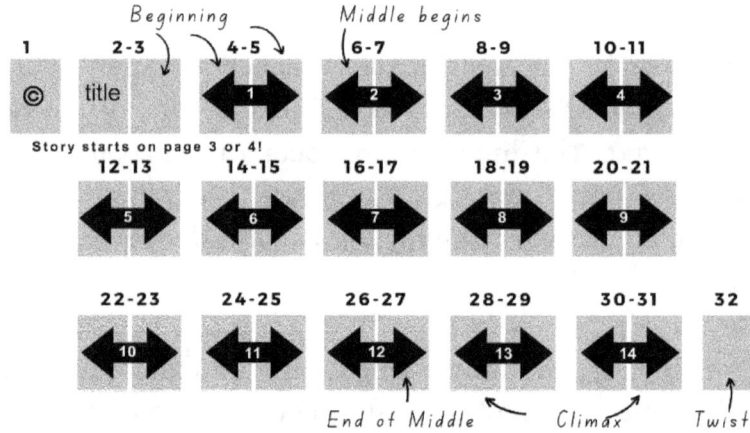

Time out, you say. What if my story needs 48 pages? Or 56?

Maybe it does. And if you're planning to self-publish, go for it. But if you're hoping to attract a traditional publisher, we think it's best to stick with the 32-page format. After you become a bestselling picture book author, you can call your own shots (!!!).

Each page is called a spread. A double page is a double spread. Write, insert, or paste your ideas or text onto each page. Play around with the format and layout – include spots (spot-light illustrations), full spreads (think: 1 page), double spreads (think: open book, 2 pages), wordless pages, and pages with text at the top and/or at the bottom. You don't have to decide everything – for example, you can leave the illustrations, font, and color schemes for later.

Remember every story has a beginning, middle, and an end. We recommend starting on page 3, a right-sided page, or page 4, a left-sided page.

> NOTE: In many finished picture books, the first 2 pages are the title and copyright pages, which is why your story will likely begin on page 3 or 4. That's not a must – but it is a sign to publishing folks that you know what you're doing.

And if any of this pagination talk is still unclear, just pull a picture book off your shelf (you probably have dozens of mentor texts, no?) and flip through it to see how they handle their layout.

> Pro Tip: Remember page 32 is reserved for your clever twist.

Story Maps

For a middle grade or YA novel, our favorite tool is called a story map, which is basically a map of your scenes – even if you don't know how many you'll end up with. Remember your map is a living document that you'll fill in as you write, like an inventory.

How you generate your story map is up to you. If you're a techie at heart, you might enjoy using a software program (more info on software to follow). Old school writers stick with the tried and true: notebooks, whiteboards, index cards, and yellow stickies.

As usual, we fall in the middle. One of us maps in Word and loves index cards. The other in a spreadsheet program like Excel.

Here's the start of a story map in Excel, based on the MG novel we made up for the purposes of this book: *Agnes and Tofu and the Best Paws Detective Agency* (See Appendix). Use it as a reference as you read the step by step that follows.

Agnes and Tofu and the Best Paws Detective Agency

*M – Main Character, A – Antagonist

Act 1					
Scene 1	Who?	Where?	Want?	What happens?	Change?
Opening Scene	Agnes (M)	Library	To make friends	Agnes meets Tofu. Figures out what he's trying to tell her.	Agnes decides a dog walking business is the way to make friends
	Tofu (M)		For Agnes to help him escape circus workers		Tofu "convinces" Agnes to take him home
Scene 2	Who?	Where?	Want?	What happens?	Change?
	Agnes (M)	Kitchen	To get permission from Mom	Agnes tells Mom their neighbor's pitbull & Chihuahua never get walked. They need her!	Agnes gets Mom to agree she can walk Tofu, the pitbull, & Chihuahua on a trial basis.
	Tofu (M)		To "convince" Agnes to keep him	Tofu shows off a circus flip & knocks over Mom's coffee	
	Mom (A)		To stop Agnes from starting a dogwalking business	Mom says she's heard about dognappers. What if Agnes is mistaken for them?	
Scene 3	Who?	Where?	Want?	What happens?	Change?
	Agnes (M)	Sidewalk	To use the other dogs, Tofu & his tricks to attract more clients	While people stop to watch Tofu, Agnes hands out business cards	The pitbull & Chihuahua are stolen! Agnes & Tofu follow the van!
	Tofu (M)		To entertain everybody		
Inciting Incident (TURN #1)	Dognappers (A)		To steal the pitbull & Chihuahua	When Agnes is distracted with potential clients, they snatch the 2 dogs	

Number your scenes or chapters going down the left-hand column of your spreadsheet (or stack your notecards vertically). Make sure to include the scene's geographic location – Act 1 (Beginning), Act 2 (Middle), Act 3 (End) so you can "see" your whole story at a glance.

Across the top, make headings. Here are the headings we like (feel free to create your own): who (who are the characters in the scene); where (where does the scene take place); want (what do the protagonist and the antagonist in the scene want – spoiler alert – their wants should conflict); what happens; and change (what changes as a result of this scene). Not only do these headings guide you through your scene, but they also tell the reader what they need to know. We call this the setup. For more on information on scenes and setups, check out Session 4.

Don't forget to add your **5 Turns** in bold. Notice we did that above. (For everything you need to know about turns, check out Session 3, This is How WE Do It.) We like to use block color-coding, but since our example is black & white, you'll have to use your imagination!

Vision Boards

Just like a regular vision board, a vision board for your story is a physical or digital board where you add whatever helps you "see" your vision. Think: doodles, images, or sketches and/or tack on icons, stickers, graphics, maps, and photos.

An easy place to start is with your story's world. Download or cut out photos that reflect the time and place of your story. Locate maps and copy them. Clip pics that reflect the fashion, morals, and customs. Move on to the 12 adjectives (each) that describe your main character and antagonist. For more info on the 12 adjectives, check out Session 3.

The content – virtual, physical, or in between – is limited only by your imagination. Remember vision boards aren't just for world-building. Of course, they're awesome for that, too.

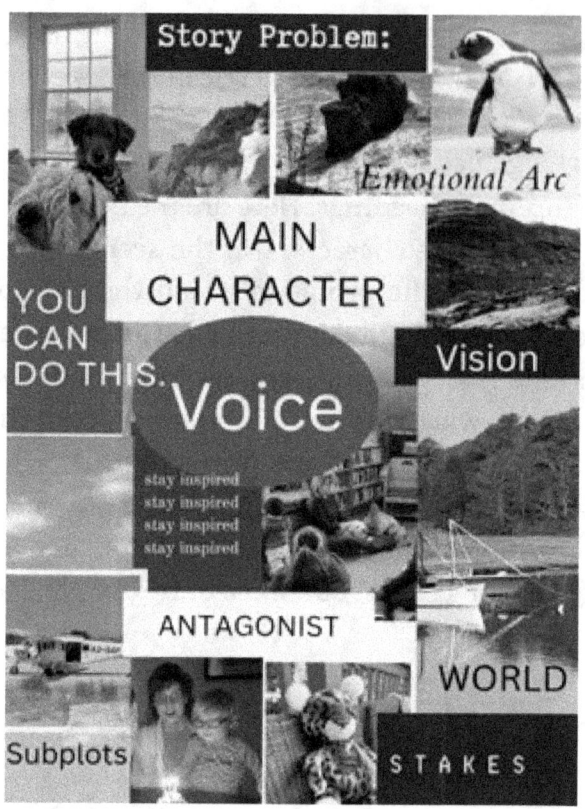

Digital Functionality/Organization

Software programs are perhaps the most available tools of all and the hardest to evaluate. Literally, there are so many to choose from!

For techies, we suggest programs with easy-to-use features specific to writing and editing like: word processing, file organization, grammar-checks, spell-checks, plagiarism-checks, collaboration opportunities (if that makes sense), usability across devices, distraction assistance, cloud storage, automatic saving, and lost draft retrieval.

(Whew, let us catch our breath!)

Popular products include: *Scrivener, Google Docs, ProWritingAid, NovelPad, Reedsy Book Editor, Squibler, Microsoft Word,* and *Grammarly.* If any seem like a good fit, sign up for a free trial or dive in.

One of us loves *Final Draft,* a subscription service aimed at screenwriting that transitions well to novel writing, and which offers a broad range of options for storage, outlining, character development, multi-screen formats, and automatic formatting (good for graphic novels).

Tons of our writing colleagues use writing software. If you find a program you like, we'd love to hear about it!

If you're not a techie – you'd rather take one of those polar plunges than learn how to use ANY new software – there are still tools out there just for you. First off, start with the basic platforms – Microsoft and Apple – and use them to make notes and story maps. We use them all the time – printing lists that we then paste in our notebooks or pin to a board. The point is that taking notes and saving them is itself a valuable tool.

So is switching between media. First create your notes on your laptop, then journal in your notebook longhand. Or longhand, interview your main character, then create a color-coded spreadsheet or picture book dummy. Creating lists and notes generates documents that you can print out and tape somewhere that you'll look at every day – ie, keep your thoughts and notes front and center. After all, even the most creative of us can use some help some time! Changing media can also encourage your characters to reveal themselves in new ways or create space for those aha! moments. Who doesn't love those *aha*! moments? Our point is, find your own way. Create your own process. Pick the tools you want and add them to your toolbox.

Take a Breath
Mindset, Setting Goals, and Accountability

Ah. Big inhale. We promised you a breather and here it is.

Mindset

The first mental challenge you may confront is mindset. Why? Because your frame of mind can smooth your writing path forward, or it can literally strap you into a pair of cement overshoes.

We like to think of it this way. There are 2 parts to our writing selves – the believer and the doubter. They both have roles to play, but not at the same time.

The believer is the part of you who's obsessed with your initial story idea, who believes it's 100% worth writing, who knows deep down that you're the only writer who can pull off this idea.

The believer is also the part of you who wants to keep going. Every time you sit down to write, the believer is excited to dig back in. The believer feels confident that the story is going to turn out exactly the way it should.

The doubter is just who you think it is – the you who doubts. That inner critic who whispers in your ear: *This idea is only great in your head. This story is a piece of garbage! You're not a writer. You don't have what it takes. You're not good enough.* Need we go on?

So, is it any surprise that both of you show up when you sit down to write? The trick to writing a successful 1st draft is to tune into your believer – give them wings! And muzzle your doubter. Keep them gagged THE WHOLE TIME YOU'RE WRITING. You need to believe and continue to believe in order to get that idea down on paper – for as long as it takes.

Repeat After Us...

The goal of a 1st draft is to exist.
A 1st draft won't sell the story to a publisher.
A 1st draft won't launch anyone's career as an author.
No one ever has to see the 1st draft.
A 1st draft is only the first step in getting a story onto the page.
1st drafts are not supposed to be perfect. Not even close.

Setting Goals

Have we mentioned that we're huge fans of setting goals BEFOREHAND? If you're a glass-half-full person (and even if you're not), we highly recommend creating a schedule. How is up to you.

The obvious way is to make a list of your top five wants:

I want to finish my 1st draft by year end.
I want to write 2,000 words a day.
I want to take a week off in October.
I want to attend XYZ writer's conference.
I want to...

Now incorporate those goals into a schedule – use Google calendar, an old-fashioned date book, chalk, a giant home calendar – whatever. Be as detailed as you want. Or not.

If you end up missing your goals, falling behind, or throwing your schedule in the literal or virtual trash (hey, it happens to everybody), DO give yourself permission to regroup. Take a breath. Draft a new schedule. Start again.

The goal isn't to be perfect, it's to finish.

Because seriously, the high you get from finishing a picture book or full-length novel is blow-your-mind amazing. Even if you end up rewriting your draft multiple times (BTW, you will; we do all the time), the thrill never goes away. Ever.

Accountability/Keeping on Track

Now that you've created a schedule, how do you stick to it? Because when it comes to writing a book, there's one basic truth – you will only be successful if you actually show up, do the work, and see it through to the end. The only thing that matters is that you write the words. Full stop.

So what's the best way to hold yourself accountable? Well, that depends.
Be honest about what motivates you. Pressure? Rewards? The buddy system? Something else?

Do you crave routine? Do you need to set small goals? Do you need to warm up or get into the right frame of mind each time you sit down to write? Do you need clear rewards for achieving your goals?

Be clear about what's right for you and what will fit into your life. Whatever it is, set it up.

As for us, we LOVE to phone a friend – especially if that friend is also writing. Tell your friend when or how much you plan to write, then report back.

OH and one more thing!

If your accountability method fails, make a change. As in, right away. There's no point in sticking with something that isn't helping you achieve your goals.

That's what we do. And we've been writing buddies for over 10 years!

– Session 2 –
Find Your "Just Right" Approach

There's No One Way to Write

In fact, there are as many approaches as there are writers, and sometimes writers change course from one book to the next. None of that matters in the end. All that matters is that you put words on paper. All of them.

The big question, of course, is HOW? Do you brainstorm the whole story first and write from an outline? Or do you write the story that's in your heart in some other way?

That's actually up to you. Any way that gets you going and keeps you going until the finish line is the right one for you.

That said, there are huge benefits to deciding on your "just right" approach ahead of time. The most important one, of course, is the comfort of knowing that you have a plan that will help you get back on track if – when? – you hit a roadblock.

We happen to have a favorite method for approaching our 1st drafts that BTW has allowed us to complete (and sell) many books. We are chomping at the bit to show you our way!

Smorgasbord, Anyone?

But that will have to wait, because first we want to present a buffet of approaches, from classic polar opposites – pantsing and plotting – to a rainbow of methods in between.

Ready?

Okay!

Pants-ing

Say what?

Pants-ing, or "writing by the seat of your pants," means making up the story as you go along. Wing it. Play around. Just start writing and see what happens.

Pants-ers go into the process knowing that the 1st draft is a chance to play with ideas, to figure things out in real time, to see what happens.

They don't expect they'll finish with a plot that hangs together, or pacing that works, or anything close to a strong story. They do know that the raw gems they'll uncover during the process are potential jewels that they might not have found otherwise. They'll use the 1st draft as a jumping off point to nail the characters, find the plot, and zero in on the story. And that's totally okay.

Sound appealing? Take a moment to walk in the shoes of a true pants-er. For the next 10 minutes, free-write about anything – no stopping, no editing, no rereading. After the first sentence or 2, guide your mind toward a character and a place. Write in detail. No restrictions on POV, time, or problem.

Freeing, isn't it?

If this approach feels right to you, by all means, go for it! We promise to cheer you on all the way.

Plotting

Plotters – aka outliners – start by breaking their story down into smaller parts, like acts (1, 2, and 3), chapters/scenes/spreads, and filling it in from there. What will happen? When? Why? They brainstorm and brainstorm until they've got it all down in outline form.

Once plotters have that outline, they use it as a guide to write their draft. As in, each time they sit down, they know exactly what they're going to write. Sound helpful? An outline can be as detailed as you want, and as long or as short as you want. It's just for you! Heck, there is no such thing as the outline police.

What if this is your story?

Jack's mother traded their cow for some magic . . . tomatoes. Horrified, Jack tosses the tomatoes into a pot on the stove.

To begin your outline, start brainstorming the characters and important story elements – Jack, Mom, the magic tomatoes, and the sauce, as well as what will happen in the first 5 scenes (or picture book spreads). Plug this info into outline form. Hammer out the next 5, then the 5 after that, and so on.

How does this approach feel?

Don't forget, even detailed outlines can be living documents. You don't have to nail your elements right away. Change is better than normal – it's good.

Let Your Character Lead the Way

Another approach is to do a deep dive on your main character. Who are they? What is their life like? What do they want? Why do they want it? And what will happen if they don't get it?

Let them into your imagination. Get to know them. What do they sound like? What do they have to say? Do some writing exercises in your character's voice. Make notes, doodle, find pictures online.

Once character-driven writers feel comfortable, they let that character suggest the story problem. Remember, the best story problem is one that challenges your character and enables them to grow.

Sound interesting? Want to practice? Choose from the following main characters:

A kid who's being bullied (cyber or IRL).
A dog who wants to be left alone.
A dragon whose wings are broken.

Jot down everything you know about them. In detail. 10 minutes of free writing. Go!

Does a story suggest itself? Do you see the first threads of the story problem? How about your main character's emotional want/unspoken story question? (More on unspoken story questions in Session 3.) How does this approach feel? If it seems like a good fit, keep going!

Allow yourself tons of room to be creative in the process. Don't even think about structure – no opening scenes, no inciting incidents. Let insights pop into your writing. Pepper your scenes with details. Immerse yourself in the character and their world. Where is your character now, BTW? Are they in the same place as where you started? In a setting that feels authentic to the story problem? Or have you veered from your original story idea? No worries if you have! Let your process be organic.

Discover more and more about your character as you write. Maybe you know they make rash decisions, but it's only when you're neck-deep in the story that you learn what kinds of rash decisions they make, why they do it, and how those rash decisions complicate things. Get it?

Z to A

Here's a question most writers don't ask enough – Do you need to write your story in chronological order?

Answer: No.

Some writers write scenes based on where their passion lies that day, according to their energy or emotions. With this approach, writers tend to write the anchor scenes first – your opening scene, your last scene, the midpoint. Then fill in the rest.

Say you're writing a lyrical picture book or a story with rhythmic language. Try working on the spread that you're feeling that day. Don't worry what comes before or after. Fiddle around with the scene that's speaking to you. The rest can come later.

Stack similar scenes and write them all in the same week. The big emotional ones, the quiet scenes, the big action scenes. The ones that are dialogue-heavy or descriptive-heavy. You get the idea.

Or start with the ending and write backwards. As long as it adds up to a whole story, that's what counts, right?

A Picture is Worth...

Drawing, doodling, or gathering images can help you visualize your story before or as you write it.

Here's how it works.

Decide on your story problem, character, and setting/world. Draw or find visuals. Notice the details in your pictures. Who and what else shows up? And more importantly, why? Use this process to flesh out your character and their world. Ask yourself questions, then fill in the answers with pictures. Draw your character as they are at the beginning. What are they wearing? Who are they with? What are they doing? Draw who they become by the end, maybe with even more detail. Then doodle the kind of story that would give the character the experiences that can get them from that beginning to that end. Do these thumbnails one at a time. Keep asking, what happens next? What does the character do next?

You can create story visuals as part of your prep before you write. Or you can do them as you write each scene or spread.

In a Jiffy

This last method is called "fast drafting," and that pretty much sums it up. Zero in on your story by creating a pitch (think: character, conflict, stakes).

Here's an idea:
Agnes will do anything to find a friend.

Noodle around with it.

Agnes gets along with animals better than people. Agnes decides to start a dog walking business.

Noodle around some more, until it feels right. Trust us, it sounds easy until you try it!

Agnes never dreamed she would rescue anyone until she meets an ex-circus Dachshund named Tofu.

Next, expand your pitch by hammering out the major plot points. Make up goals, conflict, stakes, arcs, and turning points as you go along. String these together into a summary.

A quirky girl named Agnes starts a dog-walking business, and her first clients, a pitbull and a Chihuahua, are kidnapped. She must get them back! Agnes meets Tofu, a Daschund on the run from the circus. He tries to teach her some circus tricks. Agnes and Tofu chase the kidnappers' van to the Happy Tails Rescue Shelter. Shocked, Agnes and Tofu sneak into the office and discover that the kidnapped dogs are being sold to the very same circus! The owner nabs the pair. Tofu is thrown into a kennel, and Agnes ends up back home, grounded by her horrified parents! Stuck in her room, she realizes she must rescue Tofu, or she'll never see him again. After stealing her mom's camera and sneaking back into Happy Tails, Agnes snaps pics of the owner, caught red-handed; but she and Tofu are trapped... until they perform a circus move and escape with proof – the photos! Agnes takes Tofu home with her for good. They open up a detective agency.

Then, sit down and "fast draft" your story, scene by scene. Think as you write. Picture each scene or spread in your mind as if you're watching a movie. Let the words fly. Don't stop and try to figure something out. If you're missing ideas or information, use placeholders. Literally write "insert more action here" or "add this guy's name later." The goal is to finish. There's plenty of time to go back and fill in the blanks.

Take a Breath
Yikes! Fear and How to Overcome It

Oh man, that was a lot. Pantsing, plotting, character writing, writing out of order, doodling, fast drafting... Good grief. We've flooded you with options and now your emotions are all over the place. Or maybe they're not. Maybe you're frozen inside. Numb. The point is . . . you're pitch plain overwhelmed. It's too hard.

Yes?

Actually, no.

We're not going to let your dream stop here.

We know, and you do too, that you're feeling this way – because soon you'll be asking yourself to write the story you've been thinking about and talking about and dreaming about.

What if you can't do it? What if this whole writing journey is a bust?

Phew! There, you said it.

That's a good thing.

Experts agree. Facing your fears is the first step to overcoming them.

We know because we've been there. When this happens, here's what we do.

6 Ways to Overcome Fear

Try one. Try all 6. Discover what works for you.

1. Affirmations

Set a timer for 10 minutes and write down as many positive "I am" statements as you can. As in, *I am capable. I am resourceful. I am determined. I am enough. I am a writer.* (Always end with that one! Every time. No exceptions). Don't stop until the timer goes off, OR just keep writing the same statement over and over. After 10 minutes, read through your list, "feeling" each statement as deeply as you can.

2. Listen to Musak

Flood your writing space with instrumental music. Lie down somewhere comfortable. Close your eyes and do your own version of "talking" to your inner critic. For example, tell them you're glad they're part of you, that you're grateful for the role they play in your life, that you honor them. THEN tell them they need to hang out and chill while you're writing. That it's not their turn. They'll get their turn when you start thinking about revision. That is, AFTER you finish your 1st draft. End your talk with gratitude. Repeat as needed.

3. Pencils Down

If fear takes over while you're in the process of writing, stop for a day. Not 2, not 12 – think: get back on the horse! (Does a more accurate cliché exist?) Chances are you've been editing yourself. So, start fresh and actually give yourself permission to write badly. Horrible grammar? Who cares? Boring dialogue? So what? Oops, you've changed your mind about x and y, and oh, yeah, z is ridiculous . . . why did you ever think it was cool? But instead of making the changes, create a list of the edits you want to make and keep track of them in a notebook or tablet. There's plenty of time to revise later. The goal is to finish. Say it again with us, THE GOAL IS TO FINISH!

4. BELIEVE

Make a sign and tack it up in a place where you will see it.

$$\boxed{\text{I BELIEVE}}$$

Yes! Just like that! (Maybe bigger!)

Believing is not about talent, oodles of free time, or your support system (although don't misunderstand us – a support system is huge). Believing in yourself is the only real need-to-have to get you to start writing AND to actually finish your 1st draft. The rest are good-to-haves, of course. But not technically necessary.

5. Zero Tolerance

Absolutely, under no circumstances – no way, no how – let someone else's negativity get in the way of your writing. If there's a person in your life who isn't supportive of your writing goals (gosh we hope not, but it happens), jot down a list of all the reasons you're not going to listen to them. For example, they don't know what's in your heart. Every writer has to begin somewhere.

Alternatively, find a way to use their negativity as fuel. As in, woah, dude, check out my big, fat, publishing deal!

6. Manifest, manifest, manifest.

Close your eyes, put on some inspiring music (not the calming instrumental music from above; something that jumpstarts your heart and your joy) and visualize yourself writing and finishing your story. Feel how incredible it will be to type, "The End." Smile! Picture holding your finished book in your hands, seeing it on a bookshelf, reading it aloud to an audience. The more clearly you can visualize your dream, the more you'll be offering to the universe, and really, the sky's the limit! Believe and achieve! (Spoiler alert: You can do it!)

– Session 3 –
This Is How WE Do It!

TA DAH! Have we mentioned how excited we are to share our approach?
Of course, we'd love it if you decide our way works for you 100%. But to be honest, our real goal is to offer it up so you can pick and choose the parts that suit you.

Our method is a mashup – part pants-ing, part plotting, part-everything else – with a strong push toward brainstorming ahead of time and putting a few major stakes in the ground.

We like to describe our approach as a sketch or roadmap because we believe that if you can "see" the basic structure of your story ahead of time, 1) you won't write yourself into a corner, 2) you'll nail your pacing, and 3) you'll give yourself a solid itinerary while leaving enough room for magic and serendipity along the way – the very things that will make your story pop.

Prewriting

Spoiler! Our approach relies heavily on prewriting.
Ugh! Right? We see you out there, rolling your eyes.
But hear us out.

Prewriting can be anything – think: research, character development, outlining, plotting – that helps you think about your story BEFORE you download it from your heart onto the screen/page.

ESPECIALLY your main character's voice. If nothing else, prewriting is a phenomenal opportunity to nail voice, which is a CRITICAL part of a successful manuscript.

Does your main character sound like this? "Ah, excuse me, I didn't want to bother you…" Or this? "Get out of my way, turnip-brain."

Note: We're not saying you should plan out your entire story before you sit down and write. Au contraire!

Prewriting is the planning phase where you get to brainstorm, explore, test, try, and start over again. It's also when we make notes, journal, discover, and imagine those other elements of craft, world, and storytelling that go into our actual 1st draft.

Sound like too much work? Or a way to procrastinate? Not so! We like to think of prewriting as prepping for a trip. Even if you're the most carefree traveler, you want to set your budget, book your flights, and reserve a hotel or short-term rental before you go, right? Maybe even check your passport if needed. Sure, you could also research sights, tours, activities, restaurants – you could be as detailed a planner as you want. Or not. The point is, no matter how you approach travel, you're better off if you take care of the absolute basics ahead of time.

The Big 3

Absolute basics, in our opinion, are the Big 3: Character. Story problem. And stakes. We call these The Big 3 because they form the foundation of all fiction. Without the Big 3, you don't have a story.

Here are some ways we like to flesh out The Big 3…

Character

Jot down a dozen adjectives about your main character. Include physical characteristics, important family elements – and critical socio-economic background information.

Add in their strengths in terms of abilities and personality, along with major weaknesses, both physical and internal. (More on strengths and weaknesses in The 5 Turns, below). Write down anything that seems important. There is no magic to the number 12.

If your character is a dog or a mermaid or a tennis racquet, you won't need all the same information as if your character is a human. Do your best to create a fully developed, 3D thumbnail of your hero – whoever they are.

Do the same for your MAIN ANTAGONIST. This is KEY. Without an antagonist, you don't have a story. If you have multiple antagonists (cue the cheering crowd), focus on the one that your main character will confront in the climax – whether external or internal.

BTW, you can change your mind. Play around until you settle on the exact right combination for your story.

Story Problem

Fill in the blank: More than anything, my main character wants _____. (Shocker – the blank is your story problem).

Actually, we're being a little cute here. Filling in that blank correctly could take you until the end of your 1st draft. If this happens, DO NOT despair. It means the process is working.

Now do the same for your antagonist.

Fill in the blank: More than anything, my antagonist wants _____.

But here's the ringer! Make sure your antagonist wants what your main character wants. Or your antagonist wants the opposite. The point is your main character and your antagonist must act as obstacles to each other – in a BIG way!

Here's an example of your main character and antagonist wanting the same thing:

More than anything, Voldemort wants the Sorcerer's Stone so he can return to life.
Harry Potter wants to find the Sorcerer's Stone first.

Here's an example of characters wanting the opposite:
The Grinch wants to steal Christmas.
The Whos want to celebrate Christmas.

Get it?

Stakes

Fill in the blank: If your main character doesn't achieve their goal (think: solves the story problem), _____ will happen (the consequence). The blank is what's at stake.

Stakes are what drive the reader to turn the page. A story with no stakes is a snooze. Your stakes should be age-appropriate – no Voldemort showing up in picture books (actually we take that back – might be kinda cool), and big enough to carry your story to THE END.

Check this out:
More than anything, Cara wants to buy a bag of jellybeans.
Eh? So what? There's nothing at stake.

Now this:
If Cara doesn't have a bag of jellybeans to feed to the giant jellybean monster, it will eat her instead.
Ah!

The beauty of stakes is that they can and should escalate. Life for your main character is bad. Gets worse. And truly becomes horrible from there.

Now, what if:
The price of a bag of jellybeans triples?
All the stores in Cara's town are out of jellybeans?
The giant jellybean monster hasn't eaten in five days?

The giant jellybean monster is three steps away from Cara's house?

Stakes that don't increase or (oh no!) lessen over the course of a story, are a snooze 2.0.

We're not saying that stakes have to end all life on Earth or launch a bacteria that will alter our MRNA. We are saying stakes must matter – to your main character.

With us so far?

Also, not for nothing – the story problem should connect directly to the stakes.

This is a Yes:

More than anything, Cara (main character) wants to find a bag of jellybeans (story problem) or the jellybean monster (antagonist) will eat her (connected stakes), and her whole village (better stakes), including her little sister Triesa who is too sick to go into hiding (wowzer).

Here's a No:

More than anything, Cara (main character) wants to find a bag of jellybeans (story problem) or the jellybean monster (antagonist) will eat all the corn in barn (ugh), or give up sweets (double ugh), or take up skydiving (eye roll).

The Unspoken Story Question & Emotional Arc

Okay, we said The Big 3, but really, that becomes 4 if we include your main character's emotional journey. Maybe we should call it the Big 3 with a Plus One.

Either way, the 4th foundation post of your story is the emotional void in your character's life, and how it changes BECAUSE of the story.

Not just during the story, but BECAUSE of what happens.

> NOTE: The reason we started with The Big 3 instead of The Big 4 or The Big 3 + 1 is we've discovered that sometimes it's better to hammer out the unspoken story question in revision. Not that you have to. It's just that often – like, a lot of the time – you need to finish your draft in order to wrangle this all-important concept to the ground.

> But – and we really do mean this – if you can work out your main character's emotional needs early, as in now during prewriting, you'll reap huge benefits. And who doesn't need a few bene's? Right? Not only can you incorporate your character's need into your scenes, but your 1st draft will flow more easily, and layers will appear that you didn't know existed.

Your main character's emotional arc (think: internal journey) is DIFFERENT from the action plot (think: what happens) or as we call it, the story problem. Both are critical to storytelling. Your manuscript isn't going to sizzle unless you incorporate BOTH!

You can literally research emotional arcs for like, forever, without truly gaining the ability to write them. And considering how critical they are to readers, including agents and editors – manuscripts that lack emotional depth are not likely to score a traditional publisher – this is a BIG problem. And dare we say, a HUGE reason why non-traditional forms of published fiction sell MUY fewer copies.

So, we like to make it easy.

To discover your main character's emotional need – the primary internal void in their life, fill in this blank:

What does my character hope for more than anything, whether they know it or not? _____ (the blank is the emotional need). Keep your answer internal to the character.

Harry Potter wants a family. Will Harry Potter find his family?
Fenway doesn't want to lose Hattie's love. Will Fenway lose Hattie's love?
Dario wants a friend. Will he find a friend?

Notice that we turned the emotional need into a question, which reflects the main character's journey even though it's never specifically mentioned in the text of the story. We call this the unspoken story question. And we're convinced that thinking about your character's emotional deficit in the form of a question makes the concept easier to grasp, and a total shoo-in to apply.

Simply ask yourself:

At the end of the story, will your main character be whole? Have they moved from A to B (internally)?

Then working backwards, incorporate a series of scenes into your manuscript that chronicle the change and the reasons why.

FYI. The unspoken story question is always answered in the climax, wrap up, or last scene.

Feel free to continue to nerd out about goals, arcs, stakes, story problems, and unspoken story questions in *Writing Kidlit 101*. For more on the unspoken story question, check out Session 5.

As we said above, if you truly can't settle on your main character's emotional needs now, it's okay to incorporate the need and its corollary – the unspoken story question – into your revision phase.

Just make sure that you do!

The 5 Turns

Now we want to talk turning points – those pivotal shifts in the action (think: main action plot) that keep a reader reading. But before we get to the turns, we first have to talk about structure.

Okay, we literally see you gagging.

Or yawning.

Please, stay with us!

Yes, we're certified structure nerds, but this will help tons. We promise. And it will only take a minute. Ish.

Fact: Most kidlit books utilize a 3-Act structure that equates to the beginning, middle, and end. Even picture books. Especially picture books!

And yes, we hear you! There *are* lots of alternatives. Great ones.

But we'd be misleading you if we encouraged you to use alternative structures before you've mastered the basic form of storytelling, the foundation that dominates today's marketplace.

> Here's the simple math behind the 3-Act structure:
> <u>Act 1</u> – the beginning = 25% of your word count.
> <u>Act 2</u> – the middle = 50%.
> <u>Act 3</u> – the end = the final 25%.
> No more. No less.

Okay, a few extra words here, a couple of pages there, or a scene or 2 before or after your mark is not going to sink your manuscript. As long as you get the idea.

Turning Points

By definition, the 3-Act structure depends on turns – moments (think: scenes) that drive the story to the next act or level of emotion, commitment, intrigue, conflict, and suspense. You can probably guess how important it is to have compelling turning points in kidlit. Our readers are not only demanding, but they also have shorter attention spans than grown-ups!

Turn #1

Every story has to start somewhere, and by START we do not mean BEGIN. Stories BEGIN on the first page with the opening scene. We'll give you all the how-tos on opening scenes in Session 4, but for now, know that your story will begin on page 1. (Or page 3 if it's a picture book – remember that from earlier?)

On the other hand, a story STARTS (not begins, right?) with a happening or action or thought – let's call that an event – that "incites" the action plot. Sure, this first turn could come in your opening scene. The point is it doesn't have to. Tons of stories start in the 2nd or 3rd scene, or even as far as 1/3 into your 1st act.

Victoria's book *Fenway and Hattie* is an example of a story where Turn #1, the inciting incident – Fenway's discovery that things are missing – happens on page 1.

But remember that flood of mysterious letters in *Harry Potter*? That's a clear and concise inciting incident that happens early on, but not in the 1st scene. Without that specific event, the story doesn't start. The main character will never solve the story problem. There will be no happily ever after.

Cheryl's picture book *Dario and the Whale* has 2 main characters with parallel inciting incidents – coming to a new place. For Dario, this happens on page 3 and for the whale, on pages 4-5. If they hadn't immigrated/migrated to the same new place, their friendship story couldn't begin. Get it?

> FUN FACT: In picture books, the entire opening scene IS Act 1, typically spread over 3 – 4 total pages.

To identify your Inciting Incident, ask yourself what might happen to kick off a change in your main character's world? That's Turn #1.

If you're still having trouble with Turn #1, go back and compare your main character's world at the beginning and end of the story.

At the beginning, Cinderella wants a better life. In the end, she lives happily… well, you know. We're guessing you've thought of the royal ball as the major plot event. And you're right. Now go back in time and find the event that launches the ball.

Get it? It's the invitation.

Turn #1 is the event that LAUNCHES the main character's journey. BUT/FOR that invitation, Cinderella's story would not start. She'd still be sitting there in those cinders, feeling sorry for herself.

Turn #2

Turn #2 is the moment from which there is literally no turning back. After all the changes in their world, your main character decides to set off on a quest to solve the story problem. All systems go. Turn #2 happens in the last scene of Act 1. Without this turning point, your main character would be stuck in a changed world (Act 1) with huge stakes, a big problem – and no action.

Turn #2 could be a decision or vow or a promise. It could be Dorothy landing in Oz.

It could be Harry boarding that train to Hogwarts.

It could be the old Grinch hatching a grinchy plot on how to steal Christmas.

To think of your Turn #2, ask yourself what action will your main character take to set off on their quest (not necessarily an actual quest) to solve the story problem?

If you're still having trouble with Turn #2 (or any turn), try interviewing (or re-interviewing) your main character. Make an effort to get to know your main character and their voice. Ask them what they want. Your characters know their story. Asking them for help is an awesome way to open your mind to what's supposed to happen, not what you wish would happen.

Turn #3

Turn #3 will come at the midpoint of your book – halfway into your total word count – where the tension and conflict spike dramatically (think: stakes go way up). How does the antagonist figure into it? How does that raise the stakes? How does this change everything for the main character and their quest to solve the story problem? Maybe this moment will be a huge success for your main character that turns out to be short-lived or wishful thinking. So close, yet so far. Example: Dario and the whale "meet" but fall short of connecting.

Or it might be a true low, a real disaster.

Your main character might realize it's going to be much harder to solve the story problem than they originally thought. This failed attempt to solve the story problem (usually the 2nd attempt) makes things worse and causes the character to recommit to the goal.

Or it could be an external event that raises the stakes.

The deadline gets moved up, the detective/main character becomes the target of the bad guy (or gets accused of the crime), or they find the 2nd dead body in a murder mystery. Lots of choices!

Or... a combination of all of these!

> Pro tip: Go to the midpoint of any book and see real life examples of Turn #3 for yourself. They're always there, we promise!

No matter what event you choose, your midpoint should zing with action, tension, and conflict.

The reader gasps when Dario and the whale spy each other. Hooray - they've each made a connection! But at the same time the reader can't help but worry. How in the you-know-what can a boy and a whale become actual friends?

To come up with your Turn #3, ask yourself what action or event will happen in the middle of your story to raise the stakes for your main character and the story problem?

Turn #4

Turn #4 will occur at the 3/4 mark in your word count, which just so happens to coincide with the last scene in Act 2. Your hero has screwed up. BIG TIME. The antagonist wins. A crisis occurs (BTW, this is not the climax). To be specific, it's the second-to-last crisis. The big plan has gone wrong, and ALL IS LOST. Your main character wants to give up. They're about to throw in the towel, the sink, AND the washing machine. Nothing can save them now; their worst fear has come true.

Dorothy brings the broomstick to the Wizard, but he says he can't help her after all. She's stuck in Oz forever.

Cinderella has lost her chance with the prince. She'll never leave her sad life.

Harry gets caught breaking the rules (because Malfoy ratted him out) and is shunned by all the Gryffindors.

To figure out your Turn #4, first ensure that your main character is facing the greatest setback yet, then ask yourself: What will happen? (Hint: Think of the worst possible outcome – the one thing the main character has been dreading all along.) Screen writers call this scene "Dark Night of the Soul."

Dario gets sick and can't go to the beach. The whale looks and looks. When Dario returns, the whale is gone. (He's lost his chance at friendship!)

Dorothy leaves with the Lion, the Tinman, and the Scarecrow. They have nothing to show for their hard work. They're stuck in Oz forever, with no heart, no brains, and no courage (oh no).

Turn #5

Your last turning point – Turn #5 – is your climax, the final confrontation between your main character and your antagonist. If you skip Turn #5, your whole story adds up to a big yawn.

To think of your Turn #5, ask yourself who will your main character confront and how will they resolve the story problem as well as the unspoken story question (the emotional arc – The Big 3 +1)?

Dorothy confronts her fear of never going home and realizes the power has been inside her all along. Clicking her heels will take her home.

Cinderella confronts her stepmother/sisters by claiming the glass slipper, thereby securing her happily ever after.

Harry confronts – take your pick – Voldemort or his minion; and solves that book's story problem.

Dario brings a potential new (human) friend to the beach, where he and the whale make an even closer, even stronger connection. Dario's heart is full. The girl is wowed. (Wrap-up – The whale flips his tail. Dario says, "See you next year!")

But wait! Who is the antagonist that Dario confronts? Huge bonus points for asking! Dario's antagonist is internal (one of our favorites!) – his own self-doubt.

Your climax should be joyful to write. Because by definition, when you "know" your climax scene, everything falls into place. Your main character, antagonist, story problem, stakes, subplots, unspoken story question, and all the scenes in between lead up to this one, great moment and it all makes sense.

> Pro Tip: Remember we mentioned your main character's strengths and weaknesses? Well, Turn #5 is where they come into play. Your story will sparkle if your main character uses their strength(s) plus everything they've gained or learned over the course of the story (possibly including help from friends) to overcome their main weakness and solve the story problem at the climax.

Don't confuse the climax with the wrap up and last scene. The wrap up and last scene are when the Grinch returns what he stole and joins the Whos in celebration. It's the "now what?" of your story.

To help keep the 5 Turns straight, here's a breakdown of each act, what happens in each one, and where to place your turns. Make a copy. Post it in your workspace. You're welcome!

Act 1
- Opening Scene
- Inciting Incident - **Turn #1** (the scene that launches the story)
- Point of no return that launches Act 2 - **Turn #2**

Act 2
- A series of scenes where the character adjusts to their new situation and makes their first attempt(s) to solve the story problem (spoiler alert: the attempt(s) fail).
- Midpoint/Stakes rise - **Turn #3**
- Series of scenes where the character gets more and more desperate to solve the story problem due to the higher stakes. (Spoiler alert: These don't end in failure; they end in disaster).
- The worst possible thing happens - **Turn #4**

Act 3
- Redemption. The main character wallows in their defeat, then ultimately faces facts, and sees a way to resolve the story problem. The only thing left to do is put the new, perilous, unlikely-to-succeed plan in place.

- Scenes leading to the main character's final confrontation with the antagonist.
- Climax – Final confrontation – **Turn #5** (Spoiler: It's doozy.)
- Wrap Up.
- Final Scene.

Okay, we lied. That was probably more than a minute. Ish. But it was helpful, right? The big takeaway is that if you find your 5 Turns, you'll find your action plot. Which is HUGE!

Because now you won't stop writing after Act 1 – you already know what's going to happen in Acts 2 and 3.

And you won't get frustrated with your characters. You already know how they change. Okay, that last one might be an exaggeration. You may still get frustrated with your characters – after all, they're individuals with specific needs and wants. But here's the rub: you won't stop writing!

Just keep in mind that after each TURN, everything changes. Always. Every time.

Put it All Together

No big mystery here.

After we spend time prewriting The Big 3 (including nailing our main character's voice) and have noodled over the unspoken story question, we move on to summarizing the five turns.

> Pro tip: Try to whittle your 5 turns down to single sentences, 1 for each. Okay maybe 2 sentences per turn. No more.

Then we combine The Big 3 and the 5 Turns into bullet points that can be handwritten on the back of an envelope or fleshed out in a formal document. One of us works off an informal chart that looks something like this:

Agnes and Tofu and the Best Paws Detective Agency

<u>Main Character</u>: Agnes – quirky, always-in-trouble

<u>Antagonist</u>: Terrible Tom, owner of Happy Tails Shelter

<u>Story Problem</u>: Agnes wants to rescue her kidnapped clients.

<u>Stakes</u>: If Agnes doesn't rescue her kidnapped clients, Agnes will be blamed; the dogs will be sold to the circus. She'll never fit in, never make friends.

<u>Unspoken Story Question</u>: Will Agnes ever fit in?

<u>Act 1</u>

    Opening Scene – Quirky Agnes new to town, in the public library on the eve of the first day of school; rescues an escaped circus Dachshund, Tofu, from handlers.

    Turn #1: Inciting Incident: Agnes's first dog-walking clients are kidnapped.

    Turn # 2: Agnes and Tofu decide to rescue kidnapped clients.

<u>Act 2</u>

    Agnes and Tofu track kidnappers to shelter; talk their way in.

    Turn #3: Midpoint: Agnes and Tofu are trapped inside the office. They discover the kidnapped dogs are being sold to the circus; Escape, barely.

    Turn #4: Agnes and Tofu return to rescue the dogs. They've taken her mom's camera and shoot photos. Captured! Pics erased.

<u>Act 3</u>

    Tofu locked in kennel; Agnes under parental house arrest – nobody believes her; Aha! the photos. She comes up with a plan.

    Turn #5: Climax: Agnes downloads the photos from TT's computer while Tofu releases all the kidnapped dogs. Agnes and Tofu confront Terrible Tom.

    Wrap Up: Agnes shows photos to the police; Terrible Tom arrested.

    Last Scene: Agnes opens the Best Paws Detective Agency office in the public library – queue of peer clients.

From there, we write. That's it! That's our process.

Take a Breath
Oh No! Writer's Block

What happens when you sit down to write, and your brain starts thinking about work or school? Or kids? Or that special person?

Or maybe your brain freezes – literally the words turn to ice.

Or you spend so much time exploring mentor texts and/or your main character that you lose your flow.

We've been there! Everybody has. There's a big difference between building creative tension and building a wall. Yet we all build those walls.

The key to getting over, through, or under the wall is to be aware that we've created it ourselves. We are our own antagonists. And that means we have the power to take that wall down.

Sounds easy.

Of course, it isn't.

What's Holding You Back?

(Um, hello? What Isn't Holding You Back?)
You can't seem to get yourself going.
You don't have time.
You've got too many other priorities.
The marketplace is too competitive.
Your story isn't good enough.
You don't know how to get started.
ANSWER: Read on, McDuff.

When this happens, and it WILL, head on down to the exercises below. We use them all the time.

> Spoiler Alert: For giggles we've included a bonus in the first one. When – not if – WHEN you're called on by an agent or an editor or a friendly ear in an elevator to reveal your logline – this exercise will be the reason you crush it. As simple as it sounds, in order to sell your manuscript, you must be able to articulate what your story is about.

10 Ways to Get Unstuck

Try 1. Try all 10. Discover what works for you.

1. Find Your Logline.
Pretend that your best friend asks what you're working on. Free-write for 10 minutes (set a timer), telling them your story, specifically answering the question: what is my story about? Use any voice, any POV, any tone. Include any detail you think is relevant. Pay attention to what YOU say. Typically, these free-writing sessions reveal new ideas that catapult you back into writing.

2. Topic: YOU.
Free-write for 20 full minutes about you. No editing. No rewriting. No revising. Your childhood, your teen years, and your life today. Mention your loves, and losses, your challenges, your successes, your passions, and least faves. Include reasons. If you don't cover all the topics, don't worry. It's only 20 minutes! And this is just for you. Writing about such a familiar topic is especially productive if you find yourself in brain-freeze mode.

3. Huh?
Say you've been doing great, hitting your word count goals, sticking to your schedule. But one day you hit a wall. Your words run out. Hey, it happens. If it does, try writing, "I don't know what to write" until you do. Then ask yourself, why? What made you stop? Write about that. After 20 minutes, do stop. Then put your work away for 1 – 2 days. Not 14. When you're ready, or on day 13 even if you're not, read your own words as if the speaker is a stranger or a fictional character. Ask yourself, "What is the deal with this person?" How do they handle commitment? Stress? What do they

respond well to? What do they hate? Does an inner issue suggest itself to you? Writing about yourself is a great way to get your creative juices flowing.

4. Tried and True.

Go for a walk. Fold a load of laundry. Empty the dishwasher. Make the bed. The idea here is to get yourself moving while letting your mind wander. Once you start doing something other than writing, your always-rebellious brain will likely go back to thinking about your story, and maybe you can coax your neurons into chucking the part that's blocking you. Give it a try!

5. Talk to a Friend.

One of our faves! Hearing yourself explain what's going on in your story, describing the block (think: saying the actual words out loud) can help you figure out a way to get unblocked. And if not, your friend will probably ask you questions that will get your mind thinking in a different way.

6. Declutter

Pose your problem(s) in the form of a question. Then write down as many solutions as you possibly can, no matter how useless or impossible or silly. Once you download the obvious or non-workable answers from your head, your brain will be free to tune into the really good stuff.

7. In Character

Pretend you are your character. Journal about some aspect of their personality, their story problem, or the stakes (depending on which of these you're blocked on). Set a timer for 20 minutes and don't stop writing until the timer goes off. (Note: 20 minutes is a looooong time.) Don't edit as you write. Let your character ramble. Channel all your feelings into the character. They're working out a problem and so are you.

8. It's a Beautiful Life

Write a page about where your character might end up – physically and emotionally at the end of your story. Imagine how they've changed, how their life is better (is it?), how they're poised for a brighter future. Then work backwards. Imagine how they feel at the start, what's holding them back? Hey, maybe that's the solution to your block (wink, wink).

9. Mr. Gorbachev, Tear Down This Wall

You can't think of a twist or a hook to save your life. There's a wall between your page and your brain. And worse yet, you appear to have put up that wall yourself.

Be honest about it. Do some journaling about the wall – the reason you can't move forward. Brainstorm ways you can get past it. Come up with a list of tools you can use. For example, you might try meditation to find out what's holding you back. Or listen to a motivational podcast. Or if you haven't yet, form or join a writers' group – online or in person. To find one, google writers' groups in your local area. Vet them carefully until you find a writing buddy or buddies – folks like you who are juggling life and trying to write. Or reach out on social media. Writers love to support other writers. Find others like you. Talk through your issues. Support theirs.

10. Change of venue

If you're still "stuck" and nothing seems to be getting you "unstuck," take your laptop or notebook, and sit under a table or in a tree. Go to a cafe or the library. See what a new perspective can do for you.

Whatever you can do to grease the wheels, get over the hump, get into the groove (insert more cliches here ha,ha), is the right way to go.

- Session 4 -
Get Started

Ready to get started? So are we!

You've got your idea. You've got your approach. You've set yourself up for success in every possible way. HOORAY!

You sit down to write, all set to bang out that 1st draft, and this question floats into your mind: So how DO you actually begin a story? Do you literally write, "Once upon a time?" Does the main character give a monologue?

A quick look at mentor texts will show you there are many ways to begin a story. But we're here to make this easier for you, so here goes –

Begin your story with a scene.

Scenes hook readers. A series of scenes add up to a story. For us, opening your story with a scene is a no-brainer.

So, what exactly is a scene?

A Scene by Any Other Name...

A scene is a mini story. A manuscript – whether picture book, chapter book, or novel – is a series of scenes or mini stories, which when strung together – you pick: push, draw, lead, funnel, herd, cajole – the reader to the ending.

Also, as we said in *Writing Kidlit 101*, every scene contains at least one character with a goal, and something at stake. The middle of the scene flows with dialogue or action/conflict or more likely a combination of the 2 that leads to a new development, a change, a surprise, or a hook that drives the story forward. That's it.

> Scene = (character + goal + stakes) + (dialogue + action + conflict) → (change)

Whoops! We left something out. A scene needs one more thing – a setup. The reader needs to be able to picture the scene, like watching a video in their mind. And it's up to you, the writer, to tell them. For example, does your reader need to know that your character has just landed on a mountain of trash after falling out of a hot air balloon? Does the reader need to know the character's deadline has been moved up to five minutes from now? Or the main character is hiding behind the villain's pet armadillo?

You get the idea.

Remember the story maps in Session 2? Here's where the setup comes into play. The setup is literally the who, what, where, and/or why in each scene. You don't need all the "w's." You do need enough of them for the reader to get what's going to happen. And yes, that means that YOU need to think about those things when planning your scene – even if you're writing a picture book – so you can tell the reader.

Okay, we hear you pointing out that each scene in the average picture book is only a line or 2. Shouldn't the setup happen in the illustrations? How on earth are you supposed to include all that stuff in the text?

Yes, it's true. And yes, much of the setup will ultimately show up in the illustrations. But that doesn't mean you're off the hook. No siree. If you're submitting to an agent or editor, text-only picture book writers (think: not an author-illustrator) don't have the luxury of illustrations.

What to do? Illustration notes? Generally, no. Art direction inserted by the author is typically frowned upon.

What you CAN do is make sure your text outright incorporates or at least hints at just enough setup to make the story sing. So, don't worry about your word count at this point. After all, you're writing a 1st draft. You can cut back later.

And BTW, writing the setup in a picture book doesn't have to take up tons of words. In fact, once you get the hang of it, it won't.

Take the Grinch in his cave way up on Mt. Crumpet above Whoville. Granted, we're not Dr. Seuss, but what's to stop you from hinting at the cave in the text of your opening scene, or Mt. Crumpet, or the snow? Or all of the above?

Like so:

The Grinch leaned out of his cave and bellowed down into the snow-filled valley. "Hey you Whos down in Whoville."

Get the idea?

If you're an author-illustrator, by all means, pump those illustrations full of setup.

For all writers, take comfort in knowing that your 1st draft will go through many revisions. You'll have tons of time to cut back, add in, and make changes.

How Long is a Scene?

In a picture book, a scene is typically one or two spreads. But if you're writing a novel for middle grade or young adult readers, your scenes will obviously be much longer. How long, you ask?

That depends!

If you study mentor texts in your category and genre, you'll notice that some have long scenes while others have shorter ones. There's really no rule of thumb. Critics like to point out that if your scenes are too short, your story might read choppy. And if they're too long, the scenes might not hold your reader's attention all the way through. What to do?

Answer: Go back to your mentor texts. Get a feel for how long the author's scenes are. If it feels right, adopt a similar technique. But as always, do what works for you.

And while you're studying mentor texts, try to get a sense of how the author balances the layout. By layout we mean the mechanics of the scene, namely: how much of the scene is written as narration/description? How much is white space (silence)? How much internal dialogue (character thoughts) vs. actual dialogue, action/conflict, new information or surprise? Especially if writing in first person, your character's thoughts may overlap with narration/description.

> Pro tip: Literally go through scenes of your favorite mentor text and underline, circle, or highlight (or make notes) to see the scene's layout. It's the best way to learn!

(For a complete refresher on scenes, check out Session 9 in *Writing Kidlit 101: A Self-Guided Course*.)

How to Write a Scene

Just like there's no one right way to write a book, there's no one right way to write a scene. So maybe you won't be surprised that we're going to share a bunch of different options like we did in Session 2. Try one or 2 and see what works for you. They're all perfectly fine!

Let's start with the 2 extremes – pantsing and plotting.

Yup, the same concepts that apply to writing an entire novel can help you write your scenes.

Pantsing

Ask yourself, "what happens next?" and then write away! Make sure to include all the elements of a scene:

> Setup + (character + goal + stakes) + (dialogue + action + conflict) → (change)

Plotting

Brainstorm and outline your entire scene, starting with what your reader "needs to know" (the setup). Include what your character wants and why, what's at stake, and the key moments of the scene, in order. Don't forget that something needs to change by the end.

Either of those work for you? Great! If not, check out some other options...

Use a Mentor Text as a Template

This is literally how one of us first learned to write a scene.

Take your analysis of a favorite scene from a mentor text (see above) and turn it into a template. Here's an example of the opening scene in a totally made-up picture book:

> *"Hi, Fawn," Petunia called, flicking her black and white tail. "Today's my birthday."*
> *Fawn raised her head. "Really? What do you want for your birthday?"*
> *Petunia's gaze drifted to the silky sheen of the deer's coat. And pretty spots. Next, she looked at her own fur, which was dull and stripe-y. "I want a coat like yours."*

So your template might look like this:

Line 1: Dialogue that introduces the main and secondary character (Fawn). Include main character name (Petunia) and description (black and white tail). Add setup: birthday.
Line 2: Action and dialogue that introduces the story problem.
Lines 3 and 4: Main character's action in response. (How is a skunk going to change her stripe?)
Line 5: Dialogue that involves a change or twist.

For middle grade or YA, consider the following totally made-up template:

3 lines of narration.

Half page of dialogue.
Interior thought: What the main character wants and why.
A page of action mixed with dialogue; 5 lines of reflection (interior thought).
2 pages of dialogue mixed with action.
End with surprising new thought.

Plug your characters and ideas loosely into this or any other template – or change it up! Especially for longer chapters, don't feel restricted. Think of it as a learning tool or guide.

Moving to the Beat(s)

Here's a fan favorite. Close your eyes and imagine watching your scene as a movie. Be as detailed as you can. Then, jot down the top 3-7 things that happen in your scene. For example:

1 - Character A enters the room, angry and wanting answers from Character B.

2 - Character A searches for Character B (who is hiding under the bed).

3 - Character C enters the room, surprised to find Character A who is supposed to be somewhere else.

4 - Characters A and C argue, push and shove. In the heat of the moment, both blurt out secrets.

5 - During the "distraction," Character B sneaks out the window.

6 - Character C ultimately tells Character A that Character B is hiding under the bed.

7 – They are both surprised to find that Character B is gone.

Now, with 1-7 as a guide, write your scene, but don't feel you have to follow these beats or use them in order.

They are your safety net. If you think of something better as you write, go with that!

Tell 'Em and Then Show 'Em

Start out by literally TELLING the reader everything they "need to know" in your character's (for first person POV) or narrator's (for third person) voice. As in,

After supper, Milah and I climb into the treehouse where no one can hear us. I can't wait to find out what happened at basketball yesterday! If the coach didn't buy my excuse for missing tryouts, I'll never make the team.

Next, brainstorm the possible things that could happen in this scene, especially what might go wrong or surprises that might come up. For example:

Milah refuses to tell what happened. (Why?)
Milah twisted a wrist and left the tryout early without hearing what the coach said.
Milah says the coach was about to buy the excuse, until someone else ratted.
Milah is about to tell when someone climbs up the ladder and surprises them.
They find a threatening note stuck in the floorboards of the treehouse.

Once you come up with an option that feels like the-right-amount-of-juicy, show your reader what happens. Start with your original premise – the setup. Then let your characters loose! Keep writing until you reach some kind of ending or point where your main character wants something else.

Blurb is the Word

Write a blurb or a summary of what happens in your scene, like a mini synopsis. Example:

Petunia, the skunk, meets Fawn the deer and tells Fawn it's her birthday. When Fawn asks what she's wishing for, Petunia gazes longingly at the deer's coat. She says she wants silky fur and pretty spots like Fawn's.

Or if you're writing a longer book, something like this:

Simonita is traveling to the Field of Feathers to find the one feather that will reveal her true identity. She's discouraged that she still has so far to go. But determined! Simonita's barely gone two steps when an evil fairy named Rhuin seizes her, turns Simonita upside down, and examines her, muttering in the strange Language of Fairies. Simonita is sure she's about to be cursed. She plots an escape.

Then flesh it out with action, dialogue, thought etc. – write the scene using your favorite layout. Refer to your blurb as a guide.

One last thought – don't feel you have to wrap up your scene in a big, red bow. It's totally fine to leave the reader hanging. You can quickly catch them up at the beginning of the next scene. Make sense?

Curtain Up – Opening Scenes

Speaking of scenes, let's tackle the one that will open your story.

We're talking about the first spread in a picture book. And BTW, remember that these initial spreads are typically the entire Act 1 (if this isn't clear, go back to Session 1). In your chapter book or novel, the opening is Act 1, Chapter 1, Scene 1.

Opening scenes are scientifically proven to be the most rewritten scenes in any kidlit book. Okay, no one has proven it scientifically yet, but they will! Because it's true.

So, if you know you're going to rewrite it a bazillion times, how do you even start? What goes into the very first scene? How do you create that hook-your-reader-right-away first impression?

Your 2 biggest decisions are – 1) where does your story begin (not start)? and 2) who is the reader supposed to root for? While the second decision is (hopefully) a slam-dunk, the first one can be tricky.

Unless your story begins when your character is born (or hatched – we're not judging), it will open at a specific moment in your character's life.

> Pro tip: Always choose the moment when something changes – or the moment that directly and quickly leads to that change – a change that's going to launch your story or be the BIG PROBLEM (with stakes). Think: your character is going along, minding their own business, and then all of a sudden – POW! something happens that changes life as usual. They find out they're getting a new baby brother or sister. It's their first day of camp. They meet that cute but infuriating someone who rocks their world. Get it?

Okay, here are some guidelines for writing opening scenes.

Mr. DeMille, I'm Ready for My Close-Up

If you want your reader to care about your story, they need to care about your main character – the one they're supposed to be rooting for. Your story's opening is where the reader and main character meet, where the reader forms their first impression. So make it a good one!

Your job is to dream up an interesting scene that showcases your main character, being who they are, DOING what they do best, on the eve of the big change. In other words, a moment before the big problem.

If your main character is a runner and a marathon figures into the climax, open with that character on a training run.

If your main character is a fish out of water (you pick the context), zero in on that conflict.

Your main character is the only one in the detention room trying to study. Or your main character, the runt in a litter of puppies, barks nonstop, disturbing his sleeping siblings.

Doesn't matter if your character lives in 1936 or 2952, on Earth or on Pluton 9. This is page 1. Your reader doesn't know this character yet. Your job is to introduce them.

Okay, if you've read our first book, *Writing Kidlit 101* (and we're sure you have), this might sound like juggling 12 balls at once. After all, you have to create a 3-dimensional main character with strengths and weaknesses, a station in life, a backstory, likes and dislikes, dreams and fears – and not for nothing, a whole world. How do you show all of that in one scene?

The answer: You don't. Not yet, anyway.

For your 1st draft, we recommend focusing on your character's main positive (think: likable) strength. Bonus points if it's the same strength they will use to solve the story problem in the climax, assuming you already know what that is. If you don't, no worries. When you do come up with your climax, you can go back and highlight that strength in your opening scene (and yeah, definitely, throughout the rest of the story). That's what your 2nd draft is for.

The main takeaway for now is to think of a situation where the character is DOING SOMETHING that shows off this strength, something that's signature to their character or their passion, AND that hints at the story problem.

Sounds hard? It isn't if you really think about it.

Say your main character is a very sociable bunny who doesn't know how to hop. You might create a scene where the bunny is yucking it up with the other bunnies (his strength), then they all hop away. Unable to follow, he's left alone (story problem). This would easily lead to a change – what's he going to do about it?

> In Victoria's first book, *Fenway and Hattie*, Fenway uses his nose (strength) to investigate (signature to his character) because he wants to protect his family (story problem), and this leads to the change – his family is moving. Note: We find out later in the first scene (alas, not on page 1) that Fenway's afraid that his family will leave without him (stakes).
>
> Oh, and let's not forget that we also learn he's a dog. He lives in an apartment building, and has a family. Plus, Fenway is full of energy, action, and he's determined to find out what happened to their stuff. Which, hello! just happens to match Victoria's original 12 adjective description of Fenway's character.

Same with Book 1 of *The Hunger Games*. We meet Katniss, alone, as she wakes up, puts on her boots, and heads out to hunt. We learn that she's a master archer, the strength she will need in the climax, and she's not hunting for fun, but for duty. Her job is to provide for her family (story problem). We also discover that Katniss is hunting in secret – if caught out beyond the boundary, she'll be tossed in prison or worse (stakes). Yikes!

Do note that Suzanne Collins weaves in the change – a reference to the Reaping – in paragraph 1. That's not an accident. Consider whether you would keep reading without this hook. We're not sure if she did this in draft 1 or draft 25, but it obviously works!

Speak Easy

What about dialogue in the opening scene? If you open with your main character DOING SOMETHING, does that preclude them saying something?

No! Just the opposite. We actually recommend dialogue in your opening scene. (Note: We don't LOVE dialogue in line 1 unless you pile on the context – see the Dartagnan example below.) Do limit the number of speakers, particularly in the same conversation. Too many voices on page 1, chapter 1, can overwhelm the reader when they're trying to figure out who is who.

With 2 speaking characters, you can show contrast, relationship (friends? enemies?), the world (Are they digging a trench in the Ardennes? Hanging out in a barnyard?), the story problem (Petunia doesn't like her stripe. Earth is under attack), the unspoken story question (Do they miss their family? Want to escape abuse?), and stakes (What happens if the hero fails?).

But be careful. Dialogue is a powerful tool, particularly in your opening, so use it wisely. Make sure to immediately ground the reader with the setup – the who, what, where, when, and why.

For example, a reader will be 100% lost if the very 1st lines of your story go something like this:

"Stop," Dartagnan said.
"I beg your pardon?" the Master answered.

Who is Dartagnan? Who is the Master? Stop what? And why should we, the readers, care?

Now compare this:

"Stop!" Dartagnan grabbed the whip out of the Master's hand and wound it around his wrist, like a black charise snake. "I am the prince and I order you to stop. Do not hit that child."

"I beg your pardon?" the Master answered.

Better, right? What saves this opening dialogue is the context, the concrete information about the who (Dartagnan), what (a child is about to be whipped), where (a place where there are princes and masters), and when (the past, the future, fantasy) Okay, one vague element in your first 2 sentences is not a crime, assuming a sentence explaining *why* follows quickly.

Here's a rule we made up – and we think it's a good one. Think of your opening as a movie close-up that focuses crystal clear on 1-2 characters plus the setup before you pan out and show us the context of the wider world. Make sense?

The idea is to make the reader focus where you want them to and pick up what you want them to pick up, like you're a film director. If you can hook the audience on page 1, they'll willingly go where you lead. Just like too little information, too many characters, too many details, too much going on will be confusing. And BTW, the younger the reader, the less time you have to grab their attention before they shift over to the next toy, video game, or device.

Now Cast Your Hook!

Seriously? There's more?

Yup. Your opening MUST incorporate a hook. We hinted at it above, just like your opening is going to do. (See what we did there?)

So, what's a hook?

For the purposes of opening scenes, a hook is an "oh wow." A line, an action, or a situation that grabs the reader's attention.

Or think of it this way: a hook is the all-important change that your opening leads to. This is what we meant by opening scenes that happen a moment before the big problem. Also, DO NOT forget the stakes.

Your hook can come near the end of your 1st page, end of your 1st scene, or the end of your chapter. Better yet, drop hooks in all of the above: page 1 (preferably at the end), Scene 1 (end), and Chapter 1 (end), unless Scene 1 ends there.

> This is so important that we're going to say it again. For MG and YA novels, we recommend hooks on each of: page 1, end of Scene 1, and end of Chapter 1 (unless Scene 1 ends with Chapter 1). For Picture Books, hooks should be sprinkled liberally throughout the story, specifically on the right spread to encourage page turns.

Something along these lines:

End of page 1:

"As you wish, Prince." The Master's voice echoed with obedience, though his glare told another story. "In my next letter to your grandfather, I'll let him know you've taken in a Xhonutor child. I'm sure he'll be thrilled."

Whoa! Nasty Master, Xhonutor child, brave prince. We've got a story!

End of Scene 1:

"I want a coat like yours," Petunia says.

Now the reader is thinking: Yikes! How will a skunk change her stripe? I should turn the page.

End of Chapter 1:

Simonita had had enough of Rhuin and her poking and prodding and muttering in the old language. There was only one way to get out of the situation without being cursed. And that was to trick the fairy. "Can I ask you a question?" Simonita said to the elderly sprite in her ragged clothes and patched hat.

The reader can sense the change that is coming and will keep reading.

Okay, so that has to be it, right? Time to write!

ALMOST.

Snap, Crackle, Pop

Did we mention that your opening *line* needs to grab your reader?

We cover this topic in detail in *Writing Kidlit 101,* so at the risk of repeating ourselves – okay, we are repeating ourselves – when it comes to your very 1st sentence, make it ZING. Think: active verbs, razor-sharp details, showing not telling.

NO: *Dragon noticed the candy.*
YES: *Dragon eyed the baby unicorns slurping their rainbow lollipops. Diving straight down, he plucked those lollies out of their sweet little hooves, every last one.*

NO: *Sylvie was scared when she found the body.*
YES: *Sylvie hid behind the piling, thinking only of Wei Lu, when the body floated right past her.*

NO: *Dartagnan hated the Master, now more than ever.*
YES: *Dartagnan rushed to the front of the barren classroom, and grabbed the arm of the Master, mid-swing.*

> Pro Tip: Try rewriting your opening line in multiple ways. Are any of your rewrites better than the original? When you can narrow your rewrites down to one, you've found your opening line.

Opening Scene List

To sum up:

- Open with your main character and maybe one other,
- engaged in an ACTIVITY,
- that hints at the story problem or theme,
- AND showcases your main character's significant strength and/or weakness,
- WITH ties to what's at stake,

- AND with hooks sprinkled liberally throughout,
- Add ZING.

One Last Thing – Group Therapy

So, once you've drafted your first scene, how do you know if it works? Should you ask someone for feedback?

Answer: Yes, but...

It's helpful – even necessary – to share your work-in-progress with others if and when you're ready. And we define "ready" as "when you actually need feedback."

Is that WHILE you're writing your opening? Maybe. Maybe not. Honestly, it depends.

If you truly can't tell if you're on the right track and/or feel totally stuck, then yes, share your opening scene with a friendly critiquer. But DO include a specific request that they offer suggestions, not simply general feedback, along with a promise to root for you all the way.

Of course, it goes without saying that flat out negative feedback is not helpful. Ever. At any time. End of story.

Hold on, you say.

Didn't we tell you in Session 3 that joining a critique group was a good thing – a way to get unstuck? Now, we're saying, don't share your work until you're ready?

Yes, and both are true. Sorry if that's confusing. Groups ARE an awesome way to connect with other writers, but sharing your work before you're ready can lead to endless re-writing and not moving forward. It can also lead to loss of vision, crisis of confidence (cue the comic of the writer tossing wadded paper into the trash), and the dreaded writing-by-committee.

Your 1st draft is truly your best opportunity to explore and brainstorm and try new ideas. Do you really need a critique at this point? Does it help to hear that your dialogue is too wordy or your dear friend/favorite critiquer lost interest in your story on page 2?

Writers' group or no writers' group, we think it's better to forego feedback than to solicit comments that wake up the doubter, the very part of you that you told to wait outside. We realize this is controversial. But we're pretty adamant. Your 1st draft, by definition, will need work. Lots of work. Go into it with that mindset. Resist the urge to share until you're ready.

Planning Ahead

Okay, we promised you a plan. Here it is.

No matter what your "Just Right" approach – even if you're a true pantser – we recommend starting your 1st draft by brainstorming scenes for your full picture book, chapter book, or novel. It doesn't matter how many scenes (for now) or how general or specific they are. Just get them out of your head and down on paper.

Use any of the tools mentioned in Session 1. You do you! Yellow stickies your thing? Go for it. Your brain works better with a software program? Awesome! What is a story map anyway except a list of scenes? Picture book dummies? Ditto. Include as many scenes as you can think of. Don't leave out the crucial ones. For us, that's your opening scene, closing scene, midpoint, climax, and turns at the end of Acts 1 and 2. Reduce your scenes into short (think: one sentence) concepts.

Scene 1: *Agnes meets Tofu who is hiding inside the public library, avoiding the circus workers who are looking for him.*

Scene 2: *Agnes rescues Tofu; she has an idea; to start a dog-walking business.*

If you're a pantser, you might create your list off the cuff, literally reduce your story to a list of actions, from beginning to end.

If you're a plotter or you're into our mashup approach, you've already done a ton of work. You know the 5 turns of your action plot. Include them in bold. Don't leave out the scenes in between.

BTW, how great is it that you know your main character (AND their voice), and the antagonist, and the story problem, stakes, and unspoken story question?

So great!

If you're partial to one of the other approaches, use it to generate the same kind of list of action scenes.

Remember, your list doesn't have to be complete or set in stone. In fact, expect the opposite. You're bound to come up with new hooks, twists, subplots (more on all of these in Session 5), and plot and character revelations as you write. HOORAY! APPLAUSE! That's the magic of the process. So yeah, you will absolutely add to and change this list as you write. To reiterate, that's a good thing. Because we've said it before and we'll say it again, if you can "see" your whole story – beginning, middle, and end – you are far less likely to stop writing.

Take a Breath
Later, Gator... Procrastination

Here's a quiz. Which of the following = procrastination?

> You can't meet your writing goal for today because:
> A. That basket of laundry cannot wait until tomorrow. Cue the princess sitting on top of a wavering stack of bare mattresses.
> B. The run to the grocery store must happen now, before you write another word. And then, gosh, it's too late to write when you get back.
> C. You legitimately HATE your previous 6 scenes.
> D. A and B.
> E. B and C.
> F. A and C.
> G. C and D.

Can you see what we've done here? One of us can think of a million ways to waste time. (BTW, the answer is G, meaning all of the above). The point is we writers are experts at coming up with ways NOT to write (think: make forward progress), the most common of which is self-editing and rewriting. Think about it. Do you HAVE to rework your opening now? Your middle? Your ending?

Answer: No. Your 1st draft is almost always NOT THAT TIME.

When you find yourself doing everything "but" writing, try any or all of these 4 strategies to say "Later, Gator" to procrastination:

1. Pick a Scene, Any Scene.

Sometimes writing a scene out of sequence will help you get back on track. So, choose any scene from your list and write the setup. Don't dwell on the details. Or chronological placement. Don't worry about the final product. Write the where, who, what, and the change off the top of your head. Now set a timer for 10 minutes and write the actual scene. Go! Do not stop writing until the buzzer goes off. If the scene isn't finished, reset the buzzer for another 10 min. And another 10, if necessary. 30 min of free writing should be enough to get the rudiments down on the page. We're not talking good. We're talking lousy and sloppy. DO try to incorporate dialogue, description, internal thought, and action. DO NOT review what you've written until you've finished. The idea is to spark you into picking up where you left off.

2. Interview your main character.

We've mentioned this technique multiple times now for a reason. It WORKS! After all, you love this character! Interview them for the local elementary school paper. About their award-winning essay. As if you were the host on a talk show. Better yet, write their future college application essay – why they want to attend XYZ University, why XYZ University should admit them to the next or future freshman class. They are so deserving of your attention; how can you leave them hanging on page x?

3. Trip of a Lifetime.

Pack your imaginary bags and take your main character on a bucket list trip. Doesn't have to be to a place connected to your story. Or it can be. And guess what? You're paying! Together with your main character, decide on logistics: Where will you go? Why? How will you get there? Where will you stay? What does your main character want to do or see? Why? A creative interlude or a day to yourselves might be just the "ticket" to pull you back into your story.

4. Someone Special.

Introduce your main character to someone or something special in your life. Your partner. A dear friend. Your pet. Write the scene in the present tense as if it's happening in real time. Use dialogue and a POV that lets you "hear" your main character's internal thoughts as they respond to the introduction. Now rewrite the scene from the perspective of your someone/something "special." Pay particular attention to your main character's thoughts, words, choices, reasons. Remembering how special your character is might send you right back to your workspace.

— Session 5 —
Keep Going

Woah! Look at you! Hopefully you've written or are writing your opening scene as you read this, which means – Hooray! – you've officially started your 1st draft.

Good for you!

Way to go!

Whatever you want to write next, do. The beginning (Act 1)? The middle (Act 2)? The end (Act 3)? Or maybe you want to write chronologically, scene by scene. If writing Scene 2 feels right, follow your instincts. The most important rule at this point is to KEEP WRITING.

All the way to THE END.

Seriously. We wish you a speedy, happy, productive, writing process.

However... if your process turns out to be messy, ugly, or includes frustrating stops and starts, to say nothing of awkward voices, random characters, and unnecessary plot lines, don't give up! In fact, we like to say no matter which approach you've chosen, a messy drafting process is a productive one. So instead of getting discouraged or stopping, believe us when we say welcome, fellow writer, to real life! You are among friends.

And yes, we know our Take a Breath sections already address common mental challenges that can hijack your writing mojo. If fear, writer's block, or procrastination kidnap your manuscript, jump back to the various sections. Do the exercises. Do them again. Push through until your baby is back on track.

But sometimes it's not YOU who's the problem!

Often – and by often we mean A LOT – issues pop up that halt your momentum or freeze you out of your story. As usual, if you can pinpoint the problem, a quick look at your mentor texts might offer a solution. But sometimes we're stumped. We have no clue what's wrong with our manuscript. We only know we can't move forward.

That's what Session 5 is all about – problem areas that stymie even the most experienced writer. As you read through this session, look for ways to improve your draft. Copy our suggested techniques. Nine times out of ten (okay, we made that statistic up, but we know it's close), fixing one or more of these issues – or just making the effort – will grease your wheels and unfreeze your story.

So you can FINISH YOUR 1st DRAFT!

Curtain Down – Closing Scenes

Here's a wild thought – after you write your opening scene, consider writing the last scene next.

Seriously? Write the closing scene before writing the whole book?

Yes! How cool is that? Super cool! Or rather, super smart. Because your ending creates a road map for your middle. Which is a huge help when you're brainstorming those in-between scenes and stringing them together in a compelling way.

For that matter, after you write your closing scene, consider staying on track and writing the rest of Act 3. Think how much easier writing your middle will be!

At a minimum (and this a PRO TIP), writing your closing scene now is a sneaky way of seeing if your opening scene "works." Because your closing scene will answer the questions: Does my story start in the right place? Does my opening give all the right cues to the reader?

And if the answers are NO and NO – despite what we said earlier – it might be worth changing the opening now.

Let's say you're writing a picture book, and your opening scene takes place on the first day of school. Your main character Javit has a secret – his toy bear, Oatmeal, is tucked in his backpack. More than anything, Javit does not want anyone to discover his secret (story problem).

Now brainstorm closing scene ideas. Here are some examples:

Javit decides to eat spaghetti. (HUH? Even if Oatmeal is discovered in the climax and all goes well, this last scene does not relate to your current opening.)

Javit successfully sneaks Oatmeal out of school and back home. (MAYBE. At least there's a connection.)

Javit finds a friend who is hiding a toy seal named Whiskers in his desk. (YES! How fun. Can't you just see the story in between?)

In case it's not obvious, the closing scene comes AFTER the climax. It's a totally separate event in the story that answers, "what now?" for your characters. This is where all the warm and fuzzies come in, or a sense of hope, or at least closure. The reader can see what life will be like for the main character now that they have learned, grown, and changed.

> NOTE: The closing scene is not the same thing as the climax, where the main character defeats the antagonist, solves the story problem, and answers the unspoken story question.

Mirror, Mirror

And that's not all – to make your closing scene pop, it helps to relate it back to your opening.

Like in Javit and Oatmeal. Create a closing that mirrors your opening.

For example, set your ending in the same place as your opening.
If your 1st scene happens in Dartagnan's classroom, close your story in the same classroom.

Or create an ending that's the opposite of your opening.

In the opening, Petunia is unhappy with her tail. In the closing, she LOVES her tail, having learned that it's exactly right for her.

Simonita's story opens with Simonita ignoring the old fairy's advice. At the end, Simonita runs into Rhuin again, but this time, Simonita values her wisdom.

Or consider ending with a similar but bigger bang than your opening.

Say you're writing a re-telling of *Goldilocks and the Three Bears* set in an urban wasteland. *Yo Bears* opens with Goldi, a hungry, homeless runaway, breaking into the Bears' apartment. After she's eaten their food, slept in their beds, and broken their chairs, they confront her. The closing scene might be Goldi, released by the forgiving bears, sharing a cache of stolen food with her little brother.

Keeping the mood, theme, or setting constant will help your reader focus on the change in your main character, which bingo! is the true end game. As we said earlier, writing a great ending is a surefire way to get your head back into your story.

Hey, just for fun, try writing 10 last lines. That's right. 10 potential last lines for your 1st draft, whether you're writing a 300-word picture book or an 80,000-word YA novel.

See what you can come up with. Now match your last lines with your first. Do any of the pairs speak to each other? Which one makes the most sense? Finding a last line that really shines can be the light that keeps you writing straight through to the end.

Invitation. Please.

So here's a question – who gets to show up in this all-important last moment? And most importantly, is it just a curtain call, or what?

Obviously, that depends.

Similar to your opening, your ending should focus on your main character plus only those characters that make sense. Don't feel the need to trot out the entire cast for one final bow.

If you're considering a closing scene where your main character is a no-show, do it for a very good reason. However, unless your main character has been eaten (!) or is otherwise totally unavailable, we can't think of many good reasons to leave them backstage.

> Pro Tip: Don't forget to give your main character a goal for the closing scene. No different from regular scenes, the last scene still needs a goal, conflict, resolution, and change. But keep the goal light. Something easy. Like a goodbye scene.

Plan it well, and your last scene will leave the reader smiling, cheering, and ordering your next book.

Get Out of Dodge

Don't go bananas. The best final scenes are short and sweet. Young readers and young adults LOVE the WHAT NOW. Keep it short, but don't skimp on the impact! Fill it with heart. Don't be that guest who doesn't know when to leave the party. All we, the readers, want are a genuine thanks, hope to see you soon, and have a great night.

Twist and Shout

Consider giving your ending a twist. Twists are a lot like hooks. Only different.

Not everyone differentiates between them. We do. Like we said in Session 4, a hook's job is to grab attention and/or drive the reader to turn the page or read the next book.

A twist's job is to surprise. In picture books, they leave the reader with a can't-even-handle-it smile.

Hook: *Baby duck pulls out book after book, refusing to go to sleep.*
Twist: *Mama duck falls asleep while baby duck reads to her.*

Hook: *The monster loses friends one by one because she eats them.*
Twist: *A new friend eats HER.*

Hook: *"Come on, Aiden. Let's go swimming tonight," Vivy said. "It's a full moon. We'll be perfectly safe."*
Twist: *Aiden is a werewolf.*

Mysteries and thrillers rely heavily on twists. Successful twists require that you lay down crucial support prior to the surprise, by hinting a few times (2 or 3x – depending on the age of your audience), in logical places throughout your book. Especially if your twist happens in your closing.

Picture Book Twists

Picture books are so amazing we decided to devote extra real estate to this classic form of twist. You know, the one that occurs on page 32. Twists are a unique aspect of the artform and a primary reason readers keep reading over and over. Get your twist right, and you'll be a Mother-May-I giant step closer to publication.

Of course, picture book hooks are important too. A hook will grab the attention of the parent or librarian who's buying the book (young kids typically don't get their way with grown-ups' wallets). Whether they show up in the concept (think: Patty the Panda Learns to Breathe – the hook is the concept: mindfulness). Or as page turns – intentional tidbits of text that the writer deliberately drops into the right spread (think: right-sided page) – hooks are integral to a successful picture book.

Building in support for the twist – 2 hints (or at least 1) of what's to come – is categorically the most important aspect of the twist. Your final reveal has to delight the listener, but upon a quick look back (because you know they're going there) feel entirely consistent with the story.

If you're writing a picture book, have fun with twists! You have so many tools at your disposal. Between plays-on-words, puns, opposites, alliteration, repetition, and good old-fashioned surprise, there's no limit to how many twists you can dream up.

Here's an inside look at how to create a picture book twist:

A family of goats includes twins that don't know the first thing about behaving. The trouble they get into builds up to total laugh-out-loud chaos.
Twist options? Try the opposite. At the end the "kids" do exactly as they're told with an even funnier outcome.

Pencil lost its best friend, Erasure. There's a refrain that shows up on every 3rd page.
Twist options? Consider a play on the repetition. Mix up the repeated words for a different outcome.

Penny the penny wants to prove her worth.
Twist? She shows the other coins that she's priceless.

Rammo wants to set a world record for... anything. After he tries and fails 3 times.
Twist? He decides he's okay being the World's Best Rammo.

So, in case we haven't hit you over the head with this, an amazing twist on the last page makes for picture book magic.

Bring in the Final Hook

Sequel hooks are tasty bits of information, dialogue, or action that leave readers drooling for the next book. If you're 100% positive your book is a series, DO pop in a sequel hook at the end.

12-year-old Dartagnan has managed to save the Pluton galaxy and defeat the war-mongering Xhonutors. Twice now, you've mentioned that Dartagnan's mother was born on the last star in the Xhonutor system. Your final scene might include that Xhonutor child, the one he saved in the opening, as a stowaway on Dartagnan's ship.

> Pro Tip: Traditional publishers tend to buy the first book in a series as a standalone (think: without a sequel) and see how it sells before they

> commit to buying the whole series. If you're trying to sell your debut book, consider leaving the sequel hook out.

Like the twist, sequel hooks need support to work. How much depends on your audience. In a middle grade or YA novel, hint at the hook at least twice (some writers prefer 3x) before rolling it out. Picture books rarely need or include sequel hooks (more on picture book sequel hooks below).

Like twists, sequel hooks should also be surprising but logical.

So don't blast off to Mars after a summer camp romance at Camp Minilowahaka. (Unless your main character happens to hail from Mars). Don't send Dartagnan to Earth if Earth has not played a role in the story. Don't have Goldi be a killer. Do have Goldi eyeing her next B&E target.

You get the idea. The best hook takes a bit of the story that was left unresolved – or that the reader THOUGHT was over – and opens up a question or problem that pulls the reader to the next book like a neo magnet.

Sequel Hooks in Picture Books.

Like we said before, picture books rarely include sequel hooks. In fact, we can't think of a single one.

The reason is obvious. Little listeners have limited attention spans. Therefore, stories that continue from book to book could easily lose their audience. That's not to say that picture book series aren't popular. Au contraire! Multiple picture books in a series can be publishing gold mines! Typically, they feature the same main character and pals (other recurring characters) as they face new but similar story problems. Often the titles refer to the main character themselves to make them easy to spot on the shelf. The *Olivia* books by Ian Falconer and *Llama, llama* stories by Ann Dewdney are fantastic examples. Repetition, consistency, and familiarity are what make a picture book series great.

Oh, And Don't Forget...

We'd be remiss if we didn't remind you to use your last scene to answer the unspoken story question, if you haven't already.

We mentioned this in Session 3, but we're saying it again. The best place to start your main character's emotional journey is in Act I, possibly Scene I or Turn #1 – the Inciting Incident.

Where you end your main character's emotional journey might be even more important. You have 3 options on where to end the arc: during the climax, in the wrap up, or in the final scene. The choice is yours. Within those parameters, you do you!

But DYK (did you know?) in a MG or YA series, your main character can and should continue to grow emotionally over the course of all the books? Which means your main character needs an emotional void in each story. AND for the series, too. Let's call the latter, the UNSPOKEN SERIES QUESTION.

The best series intertwine the 2, meaning the main character's emotional void in each of book 1, 2, 3, etc, ties in some way to their journey through the entire story. And it's not as hard as it sounds. After all, mental challenges can keep cropping up in different ways. Finding friends and families can happen over and over. Those hard-won relationships? They can and do fail, renew, and fail again.

Here are some examples of emotional arcs in individual books and related series, done right:

Unspoken story question: Will Harry find a family? His uncle? Reunite with his friends…?
Unspoken series question: Are Harry and Voldemort good and evil, respectively? Or are they the same?

Unspoken story question: Will Katniss find love with Peeta? Or Gale? Or overcome her disillusionment?
Unspoken series question: Will Katniss ever find peace?

Unspoken story question: Will Fenway save Hattie? Again? Again?
Unspoken series question: Will Fenway and Hattie get back together?

Digging Deeper – Subplots

Here's a pop quiz! Subplots are:

A. Plotlines of your story that are not the main plot.
B. Opportunities for your main character to learn and grow.
C. A vital part of any novel - even novels for kids and young adults.
D. Get tied up at the end.
E. All of the above.

Okay, you probably aced it (BTW, the answer is E). But knowing what subplots are and knowing that your story needs them doesn't necessarily mean you have a clue on how to write them. And therefore, guess what? Subplots are a huge technical issue. A great subplot makes a story. An underdeveloped subplot... well, you get it.

The best is when you successfully brainstorm or organize your subplots, BEFORE you start writing. But sometimes ideas for subplots don't come to you when you're making your initial list of scenes. They wait until you're deep in the weeds of writing or even afterward as you think about revision. So first off, don't worry if you can't think of any.

Second, it might be obvious – or it might not – but you can't create meaningful subplots until you have a good handle on your main plot, (think: action plot/story problem). Or said another way, don't put the sub before the plot. LOL!

Basically, any action line that's not part of your main plot can be its own subplot.

Gem is a 16-year-old girl whose parents are trapeze artists in their family's circus.

What's your main plot? Gem wants to be a star and perform? Or Gem falls in love with the clown? Or is there a third option? The circus runs into financial trouble and Gem, with her amazing business sense, comes up with an idea to save it?

Any 1 of these would work. Your book could be "about" any of these. Once you decide on the main plot, the other elements will be kicked to subplot status.

Here are some cool rules about subplots:

All kidlit novels include subplots. MG novels might have 1 or 2; YA readers have the capacity to follow 3 or 4. The actual number is up to you, your story, and your audience. NOTE: Picture books and early chapter books don't have subplots. (See the picture book exception to the exception below).

Subplots take up less space in your book than the main plot.

Subplots differ in priority. Some subplots are important. Others are minor. The difference is determined by how closely a particular subplot figures into the climax.

In a subplot, Gem is helping her friend, a 17-year-old clown, deal with a toxic ex.

If the main action plot centers around Gem's romance with the lion tamer's assistant, then Gem kissing the clown around the time of the climax is a big deal and deserves lots of time on the page. If Gem's controlling dad plays a role in the story, but doesn't affect the climax, the dad subplot should carry less weight.

So, no skimping on important subplots! And no droning on about minor threads that don't impact the overall story!

Exception to the Exception
Subplots in Picture Books

Do picture books have subplots? Not typically. But you may have seen PBs in your research or mentor texts where the illustrations go off on a tangent, places where the art follows a separate plot line or offers the main character a chance to grow. In that case, EUREKA, that picture book does have a subplot! Consider the mouse in *Goodnight Moon,* or Jan Brett's amazing margin illustrations that foreshadow the action on next page. But here's the deal – in picture books, the main character and the story problem are what keep readers reading. Make your main story sparkle before you consider adding "subplot-ish" illustrations, or better yet, leave that choice up to the art director and illustrator.

Another rule is that in chapter books and novels, backstory and subplots can overlap. They can also remain separate. Just because you mention that Gem likes gumdrops, doesn't mean you have to build a subplot around it.

Oh, and lastly, subplots MUST get wrapped up by the closing scene. All of them.

Ideas, Mueller? Anyone?

Where should you look for subplots?

Your Main Character's Major Flaw

Subplots are a great way to challenge your main character, so look to their weaknesses for ideas. And guess what? We're talking about a thread that will become their emotional arc or the unspoken story question. If you're mining for subplots here, make sure the secondary action line helps the main character own up to their flaw, overcome it, and grow. Bonus points if this growth (or skill) helps them solve the story problem.

Gem's flaw is that she's terrified of clowns. (We know, crazy right? She was just in love with one!) The main plot is Gem wants to be a star.
The subplot as well as the unspoken story question revolves around her overcoming her fear of clowns.

Alternatively, this is a YA romance and Gem is back in love with the clown. Past hurts are holding her back.
The subplot and unspoken story question might be that she learns to trust.

An easy way to keep track of your main plots and subplots is to literally plot them like this:

Main Plot	Flaw	Subplot
Gem wants to be a star	Gem is terrified of clowns	Gem works on overcoming her fear
Gem loves a clown	Gem was hurt in the past	Gem learns to trust

Your Main Character's Relationships

Take a look at your main character (or interview them!) with an eye to discovering which relationships – new or old – lend themselves to subplots (think: a relationship with the potential to change – as in growing, fracturing, ending, becoming toxic, becoming valuable, or challenging the main character in some way).

Your main character's relationship(s) are extremely popular (and dare we say EASY) sources of subplot material. And as always, look for opportunities to use relationship subplots as a vehicle for your character's emotional growth.

Main Plot	Relationship	Subplot
Gem wants to be a star	Dad is controlling	Gem learns to stand up to Dad
Gem loves a clown	Clown is adorable	Clown is hiding a checked (ha ha) past

Your Climax

If you know your climax before or as you're writing, you can work backward to figure out what skills, information, or tools your character will need to triumph at said climax. If it's not clear how they will gain those things in the main storyline, come up with one or more subplots to do that job for you. This is a fun way to think of subplots, because it ensures from the get-go that your subplot will tie into the main plot.

Main Plot	Climax	Subplot
Gem wants to be a star	Gem confronts her fear and she flies!	Gem befriends a child with special needs, helps make trapeze accessible
Gem loves a clown	They kiss	Gem helps him overcome his toxic relationship with his ex

3 Turns for Subplots

Remember Session 3? Unfortunately, or fortunately (if you're us!) subplots fit perfectly into the 3-Act structure.

When you know what your subplots are, jot down 3 major turning points (1 each for the beginning, middle, and end) per subplot and then incorporate them into your list of scenes and weave them into the story as you're writing. Use the guide below as a reference.

In your main plot, Gem wants to be a star on the trapeze, but Gem is also a runaway. And suppose you decide there will be a subplot where instead of befriending a child, Gem is hiding out from a slimy private detective, who always wears a blue suit, the man her parents sent to drag her home. Oh yeah, because Gem is the heir to her grandfather's fortune, not her parents.

So here's how your subplot breaks down act by act:

Act 1 (Beginning) – Gem escapes from Blue Suit Man.
Act 2 (Middle) – Gem reveals why her parents want to find her.
Act 3 (End) – Gem confronts Blue Suit Man (who turns out to have a daughter Gem's age). Playing on his "dad" qualities, Gem talks him into letting her go.

As always, if you're a pantser, let those gorgeous subplots pop up as you're writing and don't worry about them. You can flesh them out or trim them back during revision.

If you're a plotter outlining your story, plug them in where they need to go.

And if you're using our mashup model, put them in where you can see they fit. You'll work on them more in revision.

The Messy Middle

Now, let's talk about the biggest area of technical disaster, and the most significant roadblock to finishing your 1st draft.

Say, you're writing your story. You're on a roll! Until you get to the middle. Act 2. Ugh. Act 2 is sooo long. For many of us, Act 2 is where we hit a wall. Full stop.

It's not hard to see why.

In Act 1, you lay the foundation for the story problem (think: action plot and unspoken story question). If you do a decent amount of brainstorming and prewriting, you'll reach the end of Act 1 without too much difficulty, especially in a picture book.

If you write Act 3 next (see box on page 72), it contains the action-packed confrontation between main character and main antagonist, along with the scenes leading up to it, and powering down after. Climaxes tend to be easier to write because by definition there aren't as many unanswered questions – other than, of course, the biggies:

Does your main character solve the story problem?

And will your main character answer the unspoken story question?

Okay, that leaves Act 2 – which EEK – equals a full 50% of your manuscript. Daunting? Doesn't have to be. When we're stuck – and believe us, we definitely get stuck – here's what we do: We break Act 2 into 2 equal parts: Act 2A and Act 2B.

Act 2A

To figure out Act 2A, answer the following questions. Make your answers SHORT and keep in mind that in a picture book, each scene will be either: a spot, a full page, or a double spread.

What happens in the first half of Act 2?

Answer: The main character tries to solve the story problem for the first time. Brainstorm those scenes, then summarize them (see below). Remember – Act 1 is already written, including Turn #2.

Don't forget those subplots. What happens in the subplot(s) if you have them? Answer: Plug in the first turn for each. Where is up to you as long as it's near the end of Act 1 or early in Act 2A. Remember that subplots are a great way to develop the main character's unspoken story question or provide a tie into the climax.

End Act 2A with the midpoint of your action plot (Turn #3). For a refresher on midpoints, go back to Session 3.

Act 2B

From here on out – Act 2B – your stakes are raised (and they might rise again – we hope). To figure out your scenes, ask yourself the same 3 respective questions.

What happens in the second half of Act 2? Answer: Brainstorm the main character's latest and greatest attempt to solve the story problem. Make it a good one! Ramp up the tension! Turn #3 raised the stakes. How does the antagonist(s) – who's probably more powerful than ever – create obstacles for the main character, the biggest obstacles yet?

Now ask yourself, what happens next in the subplot(s) if you have them? Answer: Plug in the second turn for each subplot somewhere before the end of Act 2B.

End Act 2B with a major moment (Turn #4). This scene should be loaded with tension and conflict. After all, the main character's latest and greatest plan to solve the story problem is met with surprises, twists, and maybe even looks like it's going to succeed – until WHAM! The antagonist throws in the biggest obstacle of all (So far! Remember the climax is still to come).

If you're nerds like us, consider writing a summary of Acts 2A and 2B. Note: Summaries make awesome synopses for querying!

Summary of *Agnes and Tofu and the Best Paws Detective Agency*

Act 1 – (For reference)
    Quirky, always-in-trouble Agnes starts a dog-walking business, and her first clients, a pitbull and a Chihuahua, are kidnapped **(Turn #1)**. Together with her new friend, an ex-circus Dachshund named Tofu, she must get them back **(Turn #2)**! Tofu is always trying to teach Agnes his circus tricks.

Act 2A –
    With Tofu leading the way, Agnes tracks the kidnappers' van to the Happy Tails Rescue Shelter, where shocked, she pretends to want to adopt a dog. Really, she's scoping the place out.

Subplot A: At the shelter, a cat named Bianca is so mean she's been returned 16 times. Nobody wants her and Bianca likes it that way. Bianca is chasing a particular mouse.

Agnes sees her kidnapped clients and promises they won't be there for long.

Subplot B: Bicknell Longster is a thief working at the shelter. He follows Agnes home.

Agnes and Tofu high tail it back to the shelter – this time, with the police. Terrible Tom, the shelter owner, invites the cops in. There's no sign of the kidnapped dogs.

Agnes and Tofu manage to duck into the office where they discover the kidnapped dogs are being sold to the circus! The door slams shut (woah! It's Bicknell!), trapping them in the room with Frankie, the owner's snarling, drooling, ferocious German Shepherd. **(Midpoint – Turn #3)**

Act 2B –

Thanks to Tofu and his circus moves, Agnes tosses Frankie's favorite shredded tennis ball, giving her and Tofu time to escape. Barely!

Subplot A: Bianca the cat finds herself coming up empty time and time again.

After scooting home and stealing her mom's telephoto lens camera, Agnes and Tofu sneak back to the shelter and locate the kidnapped dogs in a secret room. She takes photos, including one of Terrible Tom grooming the Chihuahua and the pitbull, ready for sale! Terrible Tom chases them.

Agnes and Tofu race home but busy, working Mom is on a call.

Subplot B: Bicknell breaks into Agnes' house and steals the camera.

Agnes and Tofu follow him back to the shelter; fall into Terrible Tom's trap.

Subplot A: Bianca is about to catch her mouse – finally – when Tofu runs into her. Chaos ensues.

Tofu is thrown into a kennel, ready to be shipped to the circus. Terrible Tom erases the photos, drags Agnes home, and blames HER for the missing dogs. **(Turn #4)**

(If you're interested in what happens next/Act 3, check out the full story outline in the Appendix)

Take a Breath
Holy Moley, You've Written Your 1st Draft. Now What?

First of all, give yourself a pat on the back!
Or throw yourself a party. We're with you in spirit!
At a minimum, pop open your favorite beverage and raise a glass to YOU!
Include your family and friends in the celebration. Or don't.
Seriously, writing a 1st draft is HUGE! Finishing it is GALACTIC!
Think about what it took to get to this point.
You zeroed in on one of your awesome ideas for a kidlit project.
And built an authentic, relatable world! HOORAY!

Plus, get this, you found an amazing mentor text that you then deconstructed to learn how that uber-successful author wrote their scenes. HIGH FIVE!

And that was before you chose a writing process – pantser, plotter, OUR mashup (You're welcome!), or another approach –

That allowed you to create an authentic, relatable, killer-fantastic main character with a unique voice, along with their perfect foil – a worthy, 3-D antagonist.

Both of whom are totally into the story problem, which hello? came directly out of your head. Of course, you made sure that your main character will solve the story problem ... because, *duh, duh, dun* ... if they don't, the consequences are enormous. Oh and yeah, your main character is working through an emotional void that they don't fill until the climax.

Most impressive of all, you brainstormed a manuscript-worth of scenes that includes your opening, Acts 1, 2A, 2B, and 3, and closing, including turns and subplots! WOWZER!!!!

All while battling periods of writer's block, fear, and procrastination.

And finally, you wrote. And wrote. And wrote.

Sure, it's far from perfect. Sure, it needs work. But it's a 1st draft. Take a breath. The hardest part is OVER.

YOU DID IT! (Or are doing it!) How great is that? Right?

So, what's next?

We think you should take a break. A well-deserved time out to enjoy your achievement. Unlike other self-directed activities, taking time off in this context is encouraged! Give yourself permission to focus on your own wellness and life balance. Whether that means alone time, social time, spiritual time, and/or time to read, play sports, or work out – DO make time for yourself.

Don't forget to also use this time to regroup. Tend to the matters that you've neglected while you've been finishing your 1st draft. Or not. DO spend time with loved ones. We bet you beaucoup $$$ that they're just as excited as you are.

And guess what? Your manuscript needs a rest, too. Only when it's had a chance to breathe will it be ready for its next step. Don't deny your story this all-important time off.

Okay, we see you raising your hand. We hear you eager beavers asking how long your manuscript should sit. We hear you (ahem) procrastinators asking how long before you have to get back to it.

Well, it depends. If you have the energy and the brain space to dive in, wait at least a week. And if not, see how you feel in a month. Two months. Or longer!

But if you need to let it go for longer, keep your head in the game by reading other kidlit or YA books, doing more research at the library or bookstore, and/or talking shop with other writers.

Regardless of how long or short the time you give yourself, we do recommend one final step before you even THINK about your next step (REVISION).

Final step – WRITE A LETTER TO YOURSELF

Remind yourself why you wanted to write the story – this one in particular – in the first place.

Tell yourself what you love about it.

Then confess to yourself – honestly – what you suspect still needs work. Generalities are perfectly fine!

Give yourself a pep talk. Heap on all the praise you deserve (hint: A LOT). Cheer yourself on. Tell yourself that you believe in your story, you believe in yourself, and you know you can pull it off (because you can)!

Make a commitment to return to the manuscript after x amount of time. Put it in writing!

Close with kindness.

You've got this! Whenever you're ready to start brainstorming that revision, reread the letter. That's what it's for!

AND... That's a Wrap!

It's time to call yourself a writer because that's what you ARE. Banish the word "aspiring." You're now officially a DO-er! Kudos! We are so cheering for you!

If this was your "first" 1st draft, well done! We're honored to have helped you through the process.

If this was your second or third or fourth (cue the magician with the handkerchiefs), we hope it was and is your best 1st draft yet!

It goes without saying that it's a joy to share our experiences with you. Both of us have been through the drafting process numerous times and each "first" is a unique journey. We think you will discover the same as you move forward with this 1st draft and all the ones that will come next.

It's taken us years to hone our process. Not only to develop the approach we set out in Session 3, but to turn our process into a teachable concept. Most of all we hope that our approach helps you with yours.

As we said in the Intro, we're particularly proud of our Take a Breath sections. The idea of incorporating downtime into a writing course is pretty novel. Or at least we think it is. The exercises, tips, and advice in those sections came to us through years of trying different approaches, discarding the ones that didn't work for us, and starring (and using!) the ones that did.

Writer's block, fear, and procrastination affect all writers in all eras, no matter the category or the genre. Like less desirable family members, they keep showing up no matter what you say! Our hope is that the head's up we offer in Session 1, Set Yourself Up for Success, on mindset, goal setting, and accountability will launch good writing habits that keep them contained.

Areas of technical difficulty are another glitch (or ditch? Haha) in the road to success. We sincerely believe the advice, techniques, and examples in Session 5 will give you a boost when you need it most.

Our goal in this book was to help you launch your story. We hope we've done that. Our second goal, the reason we do what we do, is for you to enjoy a successful career! If we haven't said it explicitly, we're doing so now. Here's to your future!

DO keep us updated on your progress. We love to hear from you! And stay tuned for the next book in our teaching platform – *Writing Kidlit 103: Revision.*

That's it... For NOW!

Victoria & Cheryl

Appendix

Anges and Tofu and the Best Paws Detective Agency

Act 1 –

    Quirky, always-in-trouble Agnes starts a dog-walking business, and her first clients, a pitbull and a chihuahua, are kidnapped **(Turn #1).** Together with her new friend, an ex-circus Dachshund named Tofu, she must get them back **(Turn #2)**! Tofu is always trying to teach Agnes his circus tricks.

Act 2A –

    With Tofu leading the way, Agnes tracks the kidnappers' van to the Happy Tails Rescue Shelter, where shocked, she pretends to want to adopt a dog. Really, she's scoping the place out.

    Subplot A: At the shelter, a cat named Bianca is so mean she's been returned 16 times. Nobody wants her and Bianca likes it that way. Bianca is chasing a particular mouse.

    Agnes sees her kidnapped clients and promises they won't be there for long.

    Subplot B: Bicknell Longster is a thief working at the shelter. He follows Agnes home.

    Agnes and Tofu high tail it back to the shelter – this time, with the police. Terrible Tom, the shelter owner, invites the cops in. There's no sign of the kidnapped dogs.

Agnes and Tofu manage to duck into the office where they discover the kidnapped dogs are being sold to the circus! The door slams shut (woah! It's Bicknell!), trapping them in the room with Frankie, the owner's snarling, drooling, ferocious German Shepherd. **(Midpoint – Turn #3)**

Act 2B –

Thanks to Tofu and his circus moves, Agnes tosses Frankie's favorite shredded tennis ball, giving her and Tofu time to escape. Barely!

Subplot A: Bianca the cat finds herself coming up empty time and time again.

After scooting home and stealing her mom's telephoto lens camera, Agnes and Tofu sneak back to the shelter and locate the kidnapped dogs in a secret room. She takes photos, including one of Terrible Tom grooming the chihuahua and the pitbull, ready for sale! Terrible Tom chases them.

Agnes and Tofu race home but busy, working Mom is on a call.

Subplot B: Bicknell breaks into Agnes' house and steals the camera.

They chase him back to the shelter, Agnes and Tofu fall into Terrible Tom's trap.

Subplot A: Bianca is about to catch her mouse – finally – when Tofu runs into her. Chaos ensues.

Tofu is thrown into a kennel, ready to be shipped to the circus. Terrible Tom drags Agnes home and blames HER for the missing dogs. **(Turn #4)**

Act 3 –

Tofu locked in kennel; Agnes under parental house arrest – nobody believes her; Aha! the photos. She comes up with a plan.

Back at the shelter, Tofu releases all the kidnapped dogs while Agnes discovers the downloaded photos on TT's computer. Agnes and Tofu confront Terrible Tom. **(Climax – Turn #5).**

Wrap Up: Agnes shows photos to the police; Terrible Tom arrested.

Last Scene: Agnes takes Tofu, Frankie, and Bianca home; together they open the Best Paws Detective Agency in the stacks of the public library.

THE END

About the Authors

PHOTO CREDIT: KAREN WONG

Fleischman Honor Award winner **Victoria J. Coe** is the author of numerous books for children, including the uber-popular *Fenway and Hattie* series from Putnam Young Readers. A sought-after workshop presenter on POV and perspective, she created and taught a highly regarded writing course at the Cambridge Center in Harvard Square for 3 years, where she first became known for the practical "Tips and Tricks" that she now regularly shares on social media. She lives with her husband in Boston & Duxbury, MA. Visit her at victoriajcoe.com or online @victoriajcoe.

Cheryl Lawton Malone earned her MFA in Creative Writing for Young People from Lesley University, and went on to author acclaimed picture books, including *Dario and the Whale* from Albert Whitman & Co. A former teacher of Writing for Children on the college and continuing education level, Cheryl is an in-demand manuscript consultant at Grub Street Boston. She and her husband live in Newton & Martha's Vineyard, MA. Connect with her at cheryllawtonmalone.com or on twitter @MaloneLawton or Facebook.

PHOTO CREDIT: KATHY TARANTOLA

www.ingramcontent.com/pod-product-compliance
Lightning Source LLC
LaVergne TN
LVHW081543070526
838199LV00057B/3765